FRANKIE & BOBBY
GROWING UP ZAPPA

CHARLES ROBERT ZAPPA

With Bob Stannard

CRZ Publishing, LLC
Ridgewood, NJ

Charles Robert Zappa / CRZ Publishing, LLC
bob@bobzappa.com
www.bobzappa.com

Book Layout ©2013 BookDesignTemplates.com

Ordering Information:
Quantity sales. Special discounts are available on quantity purchases by corporations, associations, and others. For details, contact the "Special Sales Department" at the email address above.

Frankie and Bobby: Growing Up Zappa / Charles Robert Zappa ~ 1st ed.
ISBN 978-0-9964779-0-1

This book is dedicated to the person who has made my life far richer for being in it, my wife, Diane Ellen Papalia.

Acknowledgments:

This book is a memoir. It contains thoughts and images that describe the events that took place during a specific period in the lives of my brother Frank and me. Some names have been changed to protect the identities of individuals who played a role in those events. Dialogue that appears in the text is my best recollection of what was said. It is a work intended to help readers understand how my brother became who he was.

I also want to acknowledge the following people:

- *My late wife Marcia for the time we had together.*
- *My son Jason for enjoying as much of his uncle as circumstances allowed.*
- *Dick Barber for staying with Frank as long as he did.*
- *Bill Harris for making the journey and finding his place.*
- *Bob Stannard for his wise counsel and editorial guidance.*
- *Robert Lanni for his brilliant marketing mind, incredible optimism and infectious sense of humor.*
- *Dorri Olds for her expert editing, design and social media marketing skills.*

About Bob Stannard...

Bob Stannard is an eighth generational Vermonter. He has served in the Vermont legislature, worked as a logger, sold commercial real estate and was a lobbyist in the Vermont legislature for over twenty years.

He has written two Vermont humor books: "How to Survive the Recession – A Vermont Perspective" and "How to Survive the Recovery – A Vermont Perspective". Jeff Danziger, a nationally syndicated cartoonist, did the artwork for both books. Stannard has been a bi-monthly political columnist for the Bennington Banner and VT Digger since 1995. An accomplished harmonica player/Blues singer/song writer, he has performed with BB King, Mark Hummel, David Maxwell, John Hammond, Louisiana Red and many others (see **www.bobstannard.com**).

He is a practicing martial artist and loves to fish. Fishing was how Stannard and Bobby Zappa came together. Stannard's fishing partner, Jonathan Goldsmith a.k.a. The Most Interesting Man in the World and lifetime friend of Bobby Zappa, was responsible for uniting Stannard and Zappa.

Bob Stannard lives in Manchester, Vermont, with his wife, Alison. They have two grown children, Meredith Hairston and Wesley Stannard and four grandkids.

Email:
bob@bobstannard.com

Frankie and Bobby: Growing Up Zappa

Table of Contents:

"The Child is Father of the Man"

~ William Wordsworth, 1802

The development of all human beings is influenced by many factors—the genes from their parents, the family they grew up in, the culture that surrounds them, the time in which they were born and raised. Yet each person is an individual, unique in his or her own way.

This is the story of how one unique individual, Frank Zappa, grew up. It is told by a person who has insights into Frank that no other person could have, for he grew up right alongside of his older brother. Bob Zappa was more, though, than Frank's younger sibling. He was his best friend.

In this moving memoir, we are told stories about Frank's early years that have never been told before.

And we ask what we can learn from these stories that shed light on how Frank developed into the cultural icon he became.

We see a family beset by constant moves across country, as his father pursued vague hopes of bringing a better life to his wife and their children. We can only speculate how this affected Frank's - and Bob's - development. But one thing is certain: it underlay the bond between the two boys that was made stronger because of it. We also see young Frank's constant battle of wills with his father. And we must ask how those interactions were mirrored in the outspoken man Frank became.

It is impossible to understand with total accuracy how a child becomes an adult—how exactly the child is father of the man. Still, this book fills in many of the gaps in the Frank Zappa story and goes a long way in helping the reader understand who he was and where he came from.

Diane E. Papalia, Ph.D.
Author of:
A CHILD'S WORLD 13th Ed. ~ McGraw-Hill, Inc.

HUMAN DEVELOPMENT 13th Ed. ~ McGraw-Hill, Inc.

PSYCHOLOGY ~ McGraw-Hill, Inc.

INTRODUCTION

Frank Zappa was my big brother. Three years apart, we were best friends growing up. "Growing up Zappa" covers the times and events that Frank and I shared from the late 1940s until 1967, when I worked for him and the Mothers of Invention when they played the Garrick Theater on Bleecker Street in Greenwich Village.

We were children of the post-depression era, the cold war, and the psychedelic 1960s. We lived through the birth of the military industrial complex, racial and immigrant bigotry, and the foreshadowing of the computer age.

Over the course of those years Frank developed a uniquely charismatic personality laced with cynicism, moral authority, a wicked sense of humor, and oratory skills unmatched by his contemporaries.

I wrote this book to help clarify perceptions about Frank and to describe his childhood and early adult years.

As those who knew him personally and professionally would agree, Frank was a complex person.

My brother and I lived separate yet parallel lives. We shared unique experiences that will disappear with me unless I make these stories public. The person you know as Frank Zappa was my brother, my best friend, and my closest confidante.

But my life should not and cannot be equated with Frank's. And no one, however far removed from the original Zappa family, can claim exclusive rights to his legacy or presume that any other biography is the definitive reference to his formative years or amazing career.

It is impossible to pinpoint one single thing that may have been responsible for who he and I became as adults. Our family's frequent moves were a factor in Frank's psychological development.

Living in so many different places over such a short period of time brought many challenges. Constant upheaval was one significant factor in Frank's development.

His attitude toward life was shaped by the Cold War, the beatnik era, the age of psychedelic drugs, the "summer of free love," the Vietnam War, political assassinations, Nixon, Watergate, landing on the moon, and disco. Life was great, life was catastrophic, and life was frequently absurd.

During that time, there was a mind-numbing conformity in our society. But, Frank never went the way of the crowd. As a youngster he was smart enough to recognize what was happening in the world around him and respond to those events.

It was his ability to act, react, and speak out that set him apart. What many have wondered is how he was able to achieve that level of keen awareness at such a young age.

His insights and comments still live on in his music and all that's been documented about his life.

The influences on Frank's music are widely known. They included the French composer Edgard Varese. Frank was the first rock and roll musician to use the atonal chords and multiple rhythms that Varese used in his compositions.

No other musician during this era experimented with music the way Frank did.

His music was radical. As a result, radio programmers refused to play it. Disc jockeys did not understand it and said it had no commercial potential. It wasn't like the popular music kids were listening to back then. Many people didn't understand Frank's music but those who did became immediate and life-long fans. As proof, there are Frank Zappa fan sites all over the web.

Frank Zappa was the antithesis of pop music, which is probably why he remains popular to this day. By the late 50s and early 60s Frank knew that any teenager capable of independent thought had moved beyond their parents' music. It's true of every generation—kids don't like the music their parents listened to.

Elvis Presley's sensual hip-shaking routine terrified the parents of the kids who loved him. Frank's insight into changing musical tastes helped many musically "hungry freaks" cope with their lives. It was my brother's incredible intuition that enabled him to create a new genre of music that continues to entertain and influence so many people today.

Frank Zappa was also influenced by the folk music of Odetta, the blues of Brownie McGee and Sonny Terry, Howlin' Wolf and Screamin' J. Hawkins, the rock and roll of the Dells, the Channels, the Penguins, and the Cadillacs.

He listened to early Miles Davis and was into Ravi Shankar long before Shankar was discovered by Beatle George Harrison.

Frank's compositions and performances have been written about in countless articles, reviews, and books.

This book isn't about his music. It's about how my brother and I grew up, the events that shaped his personality, and how he lived his creative and noteworthy life.

The Frank Zappa I grew up with was an awkward, self-conscious, and marginally healthy boy who later became a genuinely kind, exceptionally funny, overly generous, and amazingly smart person whose intellect was his greatest asset and his worst enemy.

He did not suffer fools and toward the end of his life was unrepentant about what he did or said, how he'd lived his life, or how he hurt those he loved and who loved him.

His untimely death left behind a hunger for his original spirit, creative mind, independence, originality, honesty, and humor.

I still miss my brother Frankie.

Charles R. "Bobby" Zappa - New York City

CHAPTER ONE

Baltimore, MD

"I never set out to be weird. It was always other people who called me weird."

~ Frank Zappa

In 1949 Harry Truman was President and Alben Barkley was VP. Nat King Cole's "Mona Lisa" was the number one hit in 1950 and Anton Karas and Guy Lombardo "zithered" their way onto the charts with "The Third Man Theme." Time for Beany, Truth or Consequences, and the Burns and Allen Show had Americans riveted to their TVs.

Frankie and Bobby in the very beginning.

Bread was 14 cents a loaf, milk was 82 cents per gallon, the average cost of a new car was $1,750 and gas was only 20 cents a gallon. In Baltimore, Maryland, a new house went for between $9,000 and $14,000.

Aunt Mary, our mom's older sister, had a house worth more than that.

This was the period when we lived on the Army base in Edgewood, just outside of Baltimore. During the hot summer months we ran around in shorts and flimsy athletic T-shirts but whenever we went to Aunt Mary's house we had to dress up, which meant at least a shirt with a collar.

Form never gave way to function when we entered the world of Aunt Mary and Uncle Robert although I doubt Robert would have cared if we had all been naked.

Aunt Mary and Uncle Robert lived north of Baltimore's now-trendy inner harbor above the intersection of Charles Street and East Lombard Street. Farther south was Light Street, now the way to Baltimore's World Trade Center and the Aquarium.

The docks were close enough to Aunt Mary's so we could smell the mix of fish and diesel fuel that wafted toward her place. Fishing boats came in by early afternoon, and during the wet heat of summer, the air was pungent.

Mom always wanted us to look alike – notice the saddle shoes and the hair part. And Frankie's fist...

East Coast created its own ennui. Baltimore's heat is nothing like western dry heat. It's a hot, wet, fungus-spawning, rot-inspiring kind of heat. The kind of heat you want to escape from, but there is no escape. The damp, sticky heat invades your pores and there is nothing you can do about it.

It was a hot and muggy afternoon in Baltimore. We were hitting croquet balls in Aunt Mary's backyard. Frankie was winning; he always had to win. He was ten and I was seven. The brutal heat kept even us kids moving slowly.

Aunt Mary's house was a Baltimore brownstone with a small front porch and backyard. We loved going to Aunt Mary's because it was always neat and orderly and had the faint odor of kerosene. Her expensive furniture was covered with clear plastic.

I didn't know if the plastic was only there for us or if the furniture was dressed in it all the time. It was a powerful deterrent to sitting down and relaxing. On hot muggy days sweat sealed my legs to the plastic and it made a sticky squeak when you stood up.

Thanks to premature puberty, Frankie had peach fuzz on his upper lip, which later morphed into his trademark Fu Manchu mustache and bull string. His voice cracked when he spoke. By the time he was ten,

Frankie was clearly different from the rest of the kids in the Zappa family.

He was far more intelligent and psychologically advanced than me and our younger siblings Carl, four, and six-month-old Candy. As the firstborn, Frankie was also our parents' favorite. He got new clothes. I got his hand-me-downs.

That afternoon while we puttered listlessly around the yard, Mom, Dad, Aunt Mary, and Uncle Robert sat at a picnic table talking. Aunt Mary was a large woman who wore her hair pulled into a severe bun. She was always dressed up, even in the summer heat. I never saw her wear anything other than a dress and sensible shoes. No slacks or sandals.

Uncle Robert was a wiry man who chain-smoked Lucky Strike cigarettes and appeared less affected by the heat than Aunt Mary. He wore workman's clothes because he worked on the docks but I had the feeling he never put in any hard labor.

We were messing around hitting croquet balls when Frankie pissed me off. He was acting snotty so I shoved him. He pushed me back. That was it. Off we went. We started to wrestle. Dad yelled, "Oh for Christ's sake, knock it off!" but Frankie had already pushed me down.

When I tried to get up he pushed my forehead, knocking me down again. Frankie was sneaky like that. He didn't fight dirty but he was clever enough to figure out how to get the upper hand.

He knew the right moves, mental and physical, that gave him the advantage. More important, he was clever enough to give Mom and Dad the impression that he was always in the right.

I tried to trip him as he walked away but he was too quick and jumped over my foot, which made me madder. Victorious in round one, he then walked over to my croquet ball, looked at me with a smirk and kicked my ball aside. I watched it roll a few inches. Then it stopped.

"I win. You lose," he said. That was it, the last straw. I'd always looked up to my older brother and would've done anything for him but when he kicked my croquet ball, I lost it. He'd turned his back on me and was walking away. I picked up my mallet and ran after him, calling out, "FRANKIE!" When he turned around I bonked him in the forehead with the mallet. 'There,' I thought. 'I won, not you.'

Bobby with our first dog, Jerry.

Frankie went down like a sack of flour in a pizza parlor and I felt a rush of adrenalin. But my victories were always short-lived. Mom screamed, "Bobby what did you do?" Dad jumped up from his chair. He came running after me and I sensed impending doom.

I ran around the yard with the mallet in my hands, bobbing and weaving, trying to avoid my father's wrath. Mom ran over to Frankie and held him in her arms. She rocked him back and forth kissing his cheek and rubbing his forehead.

Geez. It wasn't that mighty a blow, his face wasn't even red and there wasn't any blood.

The juicy little lump forming on his forehead gave me a great deal of satisfaction. It was a lump with victory written all over it. I prayed that the swelling wouldn't go down for weeks, maybe even months. I wanted that lump on his forehead to last for an eternity.

Dad finally caught me. He grabbed my shirt and yanked the mallet out of my hands. His open palm came down hard on my backside. I felt a stinging, then his hand again, smack!

He yelled and pointed, "Goddamn it go sit under that tree and I don't want to hear one more peep out of you."

Aunt Mary was atwitter over our little dust-up, while Uncle Robert sat there smoking a Lucky Strike, probably thrilled he and Mary never had a houseful of rug-rats running around smashing each other in the head with croquet mallets.

Frankie and I had been in plenty of fights before, so Carl sat near the picnic table watching birds, while our sister Candy sat in her baby pen, with no visible reaction.

Things simmered down after a while as the omnipresent heat helped the afternoon fall back into Baltimore's summertime lethargy. I can still hear the crack of afternoon thunderstorms followed by sticky, 100-degree heat and humidity. Conflicts notwithstanding, Frankie and I spent most of our time playing and laughing.

Family Matters

Though I was only seven, I knew Mom was envious of Aunt Mary's social status and possessions. Why else would Mom have made such a fuss about how we had to dress when we went to visit? Mom made it clear that we had to make the right impression on Aunt Mary and

Uncle Robert because they were special. By implication it was clear that we were not special.

Frankie and Bobby out hunting Varmints in Edgewood.

Frankie and Bobby in Edgewood. Bobby holding his squirt
gun in his jacket pocket. Frankie looking like Alfalfa.

To make up for our lower class status, Mom tried to soften her pain in the face of life's inequities. One way that helped her cope was to drag us to Sunday mass. She believed that spiritual guidance could ease the reality of poverty and help set us kids in a good direction.

Dad usually figured out a way not to go. I never heard the reasons he gave for not going to church but his absence was noteworthy. Maybe he just wanted some quiet time on Sunday mornings without having his children around annoying him. It could have been something darker. At times Dad appeared withdrawn and distant.

He seemed more comfortable not having us bother him but Mom didn't know how to drive so Dad gave us a ride to the services and picked us up afterward. Not once did he ask us, "How was church?"

Our financial status wasn't from Dad's lack of trying. During the weekdays we saw little of him. He was gone before any of the kids woke up. We knew that Mom got up with Dad to make him breakfast before he headed off to work.

On summer weekends in Edgewood he sat at the kitchen table, smoking cigarettes and endlessly solving math puzzles.

He was not a big newspaper reader but found math puzzles and TV enjoyable. Dad was fascinated by the emerging technology of television.

On Sundays playing the role of chauffeur seemed to make Dad feel better about skipping church. It also kept Mom from complaining because at least he was participating on some level. Frank and I would've loved to skip church because it was really boring. The priest said mass in Latin so we never knew what was going on and couldn't have cared less.

It was torture to sit in the uncomfortable wooden pews when there was so much more to do elsewhere like ride our bikes or play cowboys and Indians. Spending time in church listening to a monotone voice in a foreign language just didn't cut it.

By the time we were teenagers Frank and I had left the church. But before we did we had already suffered through our Confirmation, first confession, and First Communion—all rituals that were lost on us. Notice how happy I look in my Communion suit.

Bobby in his first communion and junior milkman suit.

To serve as a reminder of the important benefits of participating in church, Mom sometimes asked a priest to come for dinner on Sunday. She continued that tradition after we moved to Monterey and then to Pacific Grove, California.

On those Sunday nights when she invited a priest over, she'd cook fried chicken with mashed potatoes, and serve that with an iceberg lettuce salad and fresh Italian bread. That Catholic-priest dinner menu never changed and Mom's tasty meals were my only positive association with church. Mom hoped that maybe those priestly dinners would help Frank and me see the errors of our ways.

Frank said, "She thinks one of us will grow up and be a priest."

I wonder how different our lives, and the lives of so many people around the world, would have been if Frank had gone into the priesthood. Stop and ponder that for a minute: Frank Zappa as Father Frank...

More Frankie and Bobby in Edgewood.
Bobby looks much cooler.

CHAPTER TWO

With Aunt Mary and Uncle Robert

"One of my favorite philosophical tenets is that people will agree with you only if they already agree with you. You do not change people's minds."

~ **Frank Zappa**

Hutzler's

Later that same summer, Frank and I went to visit Aunt Mary in Baltimore for a few days by ourselves. This was after the incident with the croquet mallet and before we left for California. Mom and Dad drove us to Baltimore with Carl and Candy in the car, handed Frank and me over to Aunt Mary, then they headed back to Edgewood.

Aunt Mary told us to put our stuff in the guest bedroom. Then she sat us down and laid out the ground rules. Breakfast would be served at 7:00 a.m. It would be over and done with by 8:00 a.m. Lunch would come at noon, and dinner at 5:30 p.m. Bedtime would be no later than 8:30 p.m. No exceptions.

Her severely pulled-back hair accentuated the tight ground rules. It was difficult to listen to what she was saying while staring at her head and wondering how and why she got that bun so tight. I imagined what it would look like if that bun exploded and had to look down so I wouldn't crack up.

Aunt Mary said we could play in the backyard but never out front on Charles Street without her. She hated the summer heat and never sat on the front porch so that translated to the chance of playing out front as zero to none.

She said, "Have a good time, boys," then added that we had to clean up after ourselves because we were not going to be waited on by her or Uncle Robert. Aunt Mary was big on obedience.

*Frankie and Bobby wearing
their "Going to Aunt Mary's" uniforms.*

We didn't know the price for non-conformity but neither Frank nor I wanted to find out.

For those few days we only saw Uncle Robert in the evenings and even then just for a few minutes. He worked long hours for a fruit company down on the docks in Baltimore. He never told us just what he did at the docks but he wasn't a man who invited questions from little kids.

Uncle Robert left in the morning before we got up and would show up at night right before our bedtime. Frank and I wondered if he changed his schedule while we were there. We guessed there was an agreement that we were Aunt Mary's responsibility and he didn't want any part of us. He wasn't unkind, he just didn't seem fond of children.

Only once during our visit did he eat dinner with us. It was the last night we were there. We overheard Aunt Mary on the telephone demanding he come home early. After dinner he hurried out the door to the backyard.

He sat in his lawn chair and lit up his Lucky Strikes as he disappeared into his own world while Frank and I helped with the dishes.

But, in spite of his reclusive behavior, I do have good memories of Uncle Robert, especially because he never disciplined us. After all, we were just his in-law's kids.

That didn't hold true for Dad's brother, Uncle Joe, and his wife Elizabeth. Frank and I thought of them as the disciplinarians. Aunt Elizabeth treated us like her kids, i.e., sternly. One of her dinner specialties was to feed our cousins and us first so she could serve the main course to the adults. We were fed her "special" corn sandwiches.

That culinary curiosity was white bread spread with mashed potatoes then sprinkled with kernels of corn. Aunt Elizabeth took great pains to carefully spread the mashed potatoes thinly over the white bread. Times were tough and she was not about to waste a lot of potatoes and corn on kids. Frank called them "soapy washcloth sandwiches."

Uncle Robert, my namesake, never told us what to do. Had he not been so busy smoking cigarettes, he might have been able to get to know us, but we liked that he never had rules. During that one visit, Frank snatched a cigarette from Uncle Robert's pack and smuggled it back to Edgewood.

When we got back to Edgewood he took a wooden kitchen match and we went out back of the house where he lit it up. He wasn't very good at it. He choked when he took his first drag and then he offered it to me, but I declined. That was his first experience with what later developed into Frank's life-long tobacco addiction. Not a good start to a very bad habit.

We wouldn't let Carl smoke until he was out of diapers.

That summer's visit allowed Aunt Mary to do pretend-parenting, while secure in the knowledge that we wouldn't be there for long. Her orderly life would've been irreparably disrupted if she and Uncle Robert had had children.

After we were gone, she could go back to her uncluttered existence. Perhaps her obsessive neatness served to make her feel safe in the world. But in spite of their financial status, our family's life seemed richer.

One day, Aunt Mary took us to lunch at Hutzler's, her favorite place in downtown Baltimore. Hutzler's was an upscale department store with a restaurant. Aunt Mary was a regular shopper there and it was considered a trendy spot and a classic Baltimore department store.

It was a trendsetter because it was the first store chain—and for years, the only chain—that did not discriminate against African-Americans.

When Aunt Mary went out in public she looked very East Coast, dressed in a hat, gloves, and a snobbish attitude. When we went out with her we had to wear a jacket, shirt and tie, long pants or knee socks and short pants with Oxford shoes.

The Maryland heat and humidity was so oppressive Frankie and I sweated through our clothes, which mattered not one bit to Aunt Mary. If we were to go out with her, then we had to look good.

Without any official parenting skills, Aunt Mary made things up as she went along. She knew how she wanted us to look and behave when we were with her, even if it meant that we were miserable. By comparison, our own mother was a lot less neurotic about what we looked like, except, of course, when we went to Baltimore.

Frankie and I went along with Aunt Mary's rules. We never considered rebelling because when she shopped at Hutzler's she sometimes bought us clothes and toys. Aunt Mary and our mom were close so she knew we didn't have much money. She seemed to like buying us stuff and we liked getting it.

That day in Hutzler's restaurant when Aunt Mary ordered food she never asked what we wanted. Instead she ordered for us. Frank and I shared a grilled cheese sandwich on toasted white bread and we each got a bowl of chicken noodle soup along with a glass of milk.

Frank and I were offended by not being asked what we'd like for lunch, but wisely held our tongues. If we cleaned our plates she said we could share a vanilla milkshake or a scoop of vanilla ice cream in a wafer cone. Just going out for lunch was already special but then getting such a tasty dessert made it all the more exciting. Our parents never had the money for such frivolities.

Frank seemed more at ease on this visit than I was. He maintained his cool in situations like going out to eat with Aunt Mary. That level of cool stayed with Frank all his life, even later when he was under great physical and emotional stress either at home or on the road. But those formative years left impressions on Frank and became sources for his strong opinions.

On that day, we felt like show-and-tell items for Aunt Mary when she spotted someone she knew. She'd introduce us as her nephews, her sister Rose Marie's boys. She never mentioned Dad.

She didn't like him. It didn't seem to matter to her what we were feeling or thinking, only that we didn't embarrass her in public. We were conditioned at that early age to try to meet her high expectations.

Aunt Mary and our mom were as close as sisters could be. When Mom married our father, Aunt Mary and the rest of Mom's family didn't approve. They felt that Mom could have done much better. Dad's family came from Partinico, Sicily, while Mom's people were from Naples. The rivalry between Sicilians and Neapolitans goes back to the 11th century. The bad blood between Mom's family and Dad's wasn't that old but it was intense.

Dad's father had been a barber in Italy. When he was sober he cut hair in Baltimore for a living. Mom's father, Grandpa Charles, owned a prosperous restaurant called "Little Charlie's" down on the docks in Baltimore. The menu was not sophisticated: Maryland pub grub food. But neither were the customers. Dockworkers, fishermen, and laborers were the regulars.

Later in our lives, Mom told us that her parents didn't like Dad because he had been married and divorced and had a daughter by his first wife, both of whom lived in North Carolina.

Dad met his first wife while he was an undergraduate at the University of North Carolina at Chapel Hill. His first child, our half-sister Ann, is now a retired teacher and a civil war reenactment buff. Frank never met her and I hadn't either until our Mom's funeral in 2006.

She came from North Carolina to be with our family. It was strange meeting a relative I had never known. She never came up in any conversation and never, to my knowledge, saw our father during our childhoods.

No one in Mom's family knew or cared anything about Ann. She was Dad's daughter and not their problem. At times I felt that Frank and I were closer to our father than to our mother, if for no other reason than there were times when we related better to him.

Aunt Mary could sense that and was not pleased. She did, however, tolerate us, because we were her sister Rose Marie's boys.

Aunt Mary wanted Mom to have quality time with Candy and Carl and figured that would only be possible without Frank and me around.

She believed Dad wasn't providing us with the kind of East Coast upbringing we needed and that Mom was too weak to stand up to Dad and ask for anything. It was during that summer visit that Frank began to form opinions about life in our family and tell me about them.

When lunch at Hutzler's was over we went back to Aunt Mary's and she instructed us to take a nap. Most places in Baltimore didn't have central air-conditioning then. Aunt Mary had electric fans but they did little but blow hot air around the room.

Before our nap we took off our Hutzler's "uniforms" and emptied the change from our pockets onto the dresser in neat little stacks according to monetary value, just the way Aunt Mary showed us: dimes in one pile, then nickels, then pennies.

We plopped down on our beds and Frank began to critique lunch. He talked about how much he disliked going to Hutzler's, and what a pain it was to be there with Aunt Mary. Those were my sentiments exactly, but I could never express myself the way Frank did. I just lay on the bed and listened to him talk.

From one day to the next he appeared to grow up. He was honest and moral, never petty or ungrateful. I marveled at his insight into the complexities of grown-up society. Frank was the deep thinker. I thought about things like what we were going to have for dinner.

CHAPTER THREE

Edgewood, MD

"It's better to have something to remember than anything to regret."

~ **Frank Zappa**

After several days of having our characters molded by Aunt Mary, Dad came and got us and took us back to our Edgewood reality.

We had moved to Edgewood from Baltimore after dad got a job in the chemical weapons section at the Edgewood Chemical Activity (ECA) Center at the Aberdeen Proving Ground in Maryland.

The Aberdeen Proving Ground is the Army's oldest active test site for developing weapons. It was established in October of 1917, about six months after the United States entered World War I.

Its mission was to provide the U.S. military with a place to design and test ordnance material.

Edgewood was chosen because it was near the East Coast industrial and shipping centers. This location allowed the military to determine how to defend the nation against sneak attacks and, if necessary, load and ship weapons to areas of conflict.

The base was divided into two sections. The northern sector was known as the Aberdeen Proving Area and the southern sector was the Edgewood Area, or the Edgewood Arsenal. Dad worked at the Edgewood Arsenal.

The German Army first used mustard gas in September of 1917 during World War I. It was the most lethal of all the poisonous chemicals used during that war. It was also the most lethal gas that was tested in Edgewood. It was almost odorless and took 12 hours to take effect.

The skin of mustard gas victims' blisters, their eyes get sore, and victims begin to vomit. Mustard gas causes internal and external bleeding and attacks the bronchial tubes, stripping off the mucous membrane.

This was extremely painful, and it usually took four or five weeks for a victim to die of mustard gas poisoning.

The center also tested methods of dispersing chemical agents. It tested and developed flame-throwers and smoke screens. It wasn't the kind of place where parents felt comfortable letting their children play outdoors, especially on windy days.

Around this same time, the Naval Medical Research Institute at the National Naval Medical Center in Bethesda, Maryland was experimenting with mind-altering drugs. In 1951 they conducted a study on the effects of lysergic acid diethyl amide (LSD-25) on five "normal" subjects and 15 patients with severe depression.

Thirteen years later other studies were conducted at the Arsenal by the Psychopharmacology Branch of the Clinical Research Division into the use of an aerosol form of LSD-25. I used to wonder how they intended to use a spray can filled with LSD and who would actually be authorized to do that.

Throughout Frank's life he did not use drugs. He was able to tap into all of his unique creativity without the aid of chemicals. Frank once told me that he didn't want to use any mind-altering substances because he saw no point in not having control of his intellectual and emotional faculties. Maybe our early acquaintance with the dangers of LSD had its effect.

He said those who took LSD were deluded into thinking that they could achieve a higher mental state. He thought that was part of the hype that drug dealers used when they sold drugs to the flower children in the 1960's. He said they had no idea what to do with themselves other than wear bell-bottoms and let their hair grow.

Burn, Bobby, Burn

The Edgewood houses that civilian employees lived in on the base were a combination of corrugated metal and asbestos shingles on wooden frames. They had little insulation, allowing bitterly cold Maryland winters to penetrate the houses, which only added to the misfortune of living in one of these underbuilt homes.

The main source of heat for our house was a coal-burning stove in the kitchen. We had coal delivered and dumped into the basement. Either Mom or Dad would bring it up in buckets to keep the stove going.

Still hunting Varmints, but in the winter.

Once in a while Mom asked Frank and me to get some but, because she was afraid we couldn't bring up enough, she usually ended up doing it herself.

When it was bitter cold, I would sometimes stand in front of the stove's metal door to warm myself. One night I got up to go to the bathroom and then went into the kitchen to warm my hands and face. I turned around to warm my rear end and a piece of coal sparked and threw out a cinder that landed on my pajama top. They were cotton and quickly caught fire.

When I realized I was ablaze I ran screaming through the house. My father heard my screams and jumped out of bed. He put me over his knees and put out the flames with his bare hands, spanking my back and backside.

My pajamas were loose fitting and I must have run fast enough through the house because the worst that happened was my pajamas were ruined, the back of my hair got singed, and I had a slight burn on my back. I got off easy but my father's hands were blistered from the flames.

Since he worked with chemicals, Dad already had various ointments and powders at home. He covered my back with soothing lotion that cleared up the burns by morning. I have never been as smart as Frank, but I knew never to go near that stove again.

Knee Trouble

One chilly day, Frank and I were outside playing. We had our gas masks hanging at our sides. On days when the Army conducted chemical tests, Army regulations said we had to carry them.

Mom, known for getting excited when her children so much as skinned a knee, would have freaked out if either one of us came running into the house spitting up blood.

There was little hope that the gas masks would have been of much value in the event of an airborne gas accident. There was constant fear for civilian and military families living on the base that one day a container of mustard gas might rupture or an experiment would go haywire and anyone in the path of the fumes would be contaminated and, in all likelihood, die.

We never knew if the Army was more concerned about people dying or the nation finding out what was going on at this base.

If an accident occurred I doubt we would have been nimble enough to pull masks over our faces and tighten the elastic bands before the gas invaded our lungs. Over the years I've had nightmares thinking about the threat of leaked gas, and how space-alien-scary Frank looked in a gas mask.

Walking around carrying a gas mask on my hip made it hard to push away thoughts of my lungs getting seared by toxic gas. On that nippy day when Frank and I were outside playing, gas masks attached to our hips, I tripped on one of the belts that hung down from the gas mask.

I stumbled and fell. There was sharp pain in my right knee. When I stood up a wooden board was attached to my right pant leg. I looked down and realized that a nail in the board had punctured my pants and secured itself below my kneecap.

I ran screaming into the house. Mom went white when she saw blood and the board attached below my knee. Frank ran in with me. He stood there and watched as mom pulled the nail out of my leg.

Bobby as an Uber driver.

As I was screaming, I looked up into Frank's eyes. He stood motionless, expressionless. I wondered how Frank could remain so calm within the crisis.

"Frank," she hollered, "go get rubbing alcohol". With poise beyond his years, Frank looked at Mom and said, "What you need is peroxide."

He turned and headed to the bathroom and returned with a bottle of peroxide, which Mom applied to my wounded knee. I wondered how Frank knew what to use and even where the peroxide was kept.

Following Frank's instructions, Mom poured the peroxide on the puncture wound and it stung a little. I watched the peroxide as it fizzed and bubbled. Once the nail was out, the pain measurably decreased. Mom washed my knee and put a bandage over the hole.

"We'll have to get you a tetanus shot," she said.

When Dad got home, Mom told him what happened. He took me to the base doctor who looked at the wound and said that we had done the right thing by using peroxide because it had cleaned the puncture. He also said that unless the nail was rusty, which it wasn't, there was no need for a tetanus shot.

Frankie always had to lead me around by the hand although I don't know why.

Later that night, after the high emotions of the crisis had subsided and as I drifted off to sleep, I thought about how cool and nonchalant Frank had been while Mom and I were nearly hysterical. It reinforced my view of Frank as a hero.

Edgewood was taking its toll on all of us but it was hardest on Frank. He had developed asthma and the cold weather made it worse. He'd start coughing and wheezing then his face went pale.

I watched helplessly as my older brother gasped for air. Mom—and Dad when he was around—had to drop everything and take care of Frank.

These asthma attacks were terrifying and I felt so bad for him. I wished I could make him stronger and healthier but I was also in awe of how well Frank could keep his cool even during these bouts.

My stomach flipped when I watched him struggling to take in air. As brave as he was, I still saw terror in his eyes. There were no remedies for Frank's respiratory problems in those days, which only added to our parents' anxiety.

A nail in the knee, blazing pajamas, Frank's asthma, the bout of pneumonia I had that winter, and fear for Carl and Candy's future health, all contributed to Dad's decision that it was time for us to leave. The conversation about moving to California began.

CHAPTER FOUR

On The Road
To California

"My parents tried to make me go to Catholic school, too. I lasted a very short time. When the penguin came after me with a ruler, I was out of there."

~ Frank Zappa

One day in 1951 Dad came home from work and announced that one of the jobs he had applied for came through. It was a position at the Naval Post Graduate School in Monterey, California. As if that wasn't exciting enough, he said, "Kids, we are going to drive across country in our brand new 1951 Henry J."

The Henry J was a cheaply made, two-door sedan manufactured by the now defunct Kaiser-Fraser motor company. It was a little monstrosity of a vehicle, the Yugo of its day, but not as well built, nor roomy or well designed.

It had dwarf-like tailfins and the cramped and underpowered little auto made for an uncomfortably cramped ride. Dad managed to pile the roof of the car high with a rack stuffed with belongings. What a sight we must've been.

The Road Has Been Hit

On the day our journey began, California beckoned us and we headed west for the sun—optimistic and ready for a change. Dad said our trip would be filled with great adventures and we'd find our fortune in California. "Just you wait and see," he said.

Dad said it would be sunny and warm all the time and we could go to the beach whenever we wanted. He said a lot of things, mainly to keep us quiet so he could check the map while he drove. He was the navigator, the driver, and the warden.

The Henry J was the first car to use tailfins, even before
Cadillac. The neighbors were happy to see us leave.

Dad had a thing about being in control. He had to feel in control but to Frank and me it never felt like he was in control at all. Frank reacted by developing the same need to be in control.

Moving away from Maryland was our first experience leaving friends and family. It didn't feel so bad because we believed that we were going to a special, much better place, and that everyone staying behind would envy us.

I didn't have many friends to feel sorry about leaving and neither did Frank. We had each other and that was plenty.

Although we were excited about moving we could tell Mom wasn't. She was sad and scared about leaving her family, friends, and support system. Leaving for the unknown was daunting for her. She tried not to show her fears and anxieties but we could tell.

Like clowns in a circus act we piled into the Henry J. Candy was small enough to sit in front on Mom's lap, while Frank, Carl and I were cramped in the back seat. We were expected to sit there quietly while Dad drove.

Of course no one used seat belts in those days. Once we were underway Dad lit up a cigarette and billows of smoke filled the car.

It was the beginning of what would be a long, torturous trip across the U.S.

I hated the smell of cigarette smoke. In our little car one cigarette was overpowering. Because our trip began in cold weather and the heater in the Henry J could barely keep us warm, Dad wouldn't open the windows to let the smoke out.

At the time, no one had any idea how bad secondhand smoke was. Smoking was the norm and Dad's nasty habit was handed down. Frank started smoking early.

The transition from inhaling secondhand smoke to puffing on his own cigarettes wasn't a big jump. The cramped quarters, along with the suffocating odor of cigarette smoke, served as a catalyst for tension.

The thrill of the adventure was soon replaced by bickering, which escalated to arguing and near fisticuffs.

There were many times I wanted to strangle Frank. In those tight, smoke-filled quarters it was virtually impossible to get along.

When fights broke out, Dad screamed, "Knock it off!" and threatened to pull off the road. "If you don't cut it out, I'm going to pull over and take my belt off."

The removal of Dad's belt was to be avoided at all costs. The threat of the pain Frank and I knew from that belt on our backsides settled us down quickly.

It was on this journey that our intellectual and emotional development paths diverged. Frank learned quickly how to weasel out of any responsibility after causing a rumpus in the car.

He always made it look like I was the instigator and I could never defend myself against Frank's verbal agility so I got stuck with the blame.

There were times when things got out of hand and Dad unleashed his Sicilian temper. Mom tried to calm him down, but that only made him madder and he'd turn his Italian wrath on her.

Our parents never taught us their native tongue because they believed speaking another language would label us as foreigners despite the fact we were born in the U.S. Being labeled as foreigners was not something our father could tolerate.

In the 1950s and '60s Italian Americans were still under the cloud of suspicion, the kind fostered during the migration following World War I.

Thankfully, as quickly as Dad's temper flared, it settled down again but his wide mood swings kept us all on edge.

The farther away we got from Maryland, the less I thought about what we'd left behind. I focused more on what was ahead. Despite the daily psychodramas, our adventure still held excitement and promise.

Traveling across country as a family in our crappy little automobile, we learned a lot about how our parents interacted with each other, how we interacted with them, and how we children interacted with each other.

I learned so much about Frankie during that trip. The older brother I looked up to—so confident, so cool—had hidden fears and insecurities. I began to think that under that cool façade, Frank struggled with the stress of daily living much more than he let on.

Little did I know at the time how often that scenario would play out over the next ten years and how much our relocations would influence Frank's view of life and his perceptions of people we met along the way.

It's not that Frank didn't make and keep friends or care about what went on around him but problems arose because the Zappa household suffered from disorientation. Dad's frequent job changes resulted in our overload of moves and created an inherent confusion about time and places.

Maybe the moves were his way of pursuing greater job status and financial security, but the tradeoff was an ever-changing landscape of neighborhoods, churches, schools, and rules.

In the process we learned how to adapt but not without resentments. Through it all Mom and Dad did their best to hold the family together and Frank and I always had each other.

As we drove across country in that cramped metal box, each of us began to build hopes for our new life in California.

Frank was optimistic about his future because getting away from the East Coast winters meant no more suffering with asthma.

For Dad it was a chance to break away from the stifling formality of East Coast society, the judgmental and watchful eyes of relatives, and the negative perception Mom's family had about Dad and his future prospects.

He saw the East Coast as the source of our problems and the West Coast as the solution. On that point, Frank and Dad agreed. I had expectations of settling down someplace warm and staying long enough to make friends, again. I also saw this as an opportunity to finally have enough food. Being poor made the fear of not getting enough to eat a constant obsession.

Look, it's just a motel...

As we motored west along Route 66 our folks did their best to stretch their limited budget to make the trip as pleasant as possible. There were nightly cheap motel stops and all-you-can-eat restaurant meals.

Eating in those places showed us just how many ways there are to cook chicken. Calories and carbohydrates never figured into our meals; the average American never thought about such things then.

Along the way we stayed in strange places. One motel between Amarillo, Texas and Albuquerque, New Mexico on Route 66 was a landmark for travelers. The rooms were separate buildings constructed and decorated like Indian teepees.

Once inside, they were nothing more than dreary, musty rooms with chipped maple furniture, skimpy towels, and threadbare carpets. While I may have had fantasies about sleeping in a teepee, Frank saw it for what it was: a cheesy marketing gimmick for unsuspecting travelers.

Frank's derogatory comments set Dad off, "You're goddamned ungrateful and too big for your britches."

The uncertainty about his new job in Monterey and our dwindling finances put an extra burden on Dad. Outwardly he appeared to be strong, a man in charge of his own destiny, but I think he was insecure.

He seemed riddled with self-doubt perpetuated by the lack of confidence others had in him. The closer we got to California the more his mood deteriorated.

Each new day after an all-you-can-eat breakfast followed by another morning of Dad going ballistic on Frank and/or me while Mom, Carl, and Candy did their best to keep out of the line of fire, we would resume our journey westward. The trip was wearing thin on all of us, especially Dad.

He was developing a shorter fuse and we'd never known him to see so little humor in life, and be so oblivious to the feelings of everybody else.

He flew into road rage with the slightest intrusion by other drivers. He complained about the bad road signs, the hard-to-read maps, and the price of gas.

Mom did her best to keep the peace and gloss over Dad's escalating temper tantrums. We tried to take Dad's rage in stride, but Frank got to the point where he couldn't stand it anymore. He started making sarcastic cracks.

I didn't actually know what sarcasm was back then, but he would say things like, "Oh great, another cheap motel," which set Dad off. It seemed like Frank couldn't help himself from poking a stick at a wild dog just to get a reaction.

Our "Old Italian" Dad expected his kids to blindly obey him and he was hardest on Frank. By challenging Dad's behavior Frank became a threat to Dad's authority.

After each faceoff with Dad, Frank became more self-assured. I watched Frank's confidence grow into what became a firm conviction that he was always right.

The rest of us watched and tried not to make eye contact with either of them. We had been driving for days on Route 66 and it seemed like we'd never get to California.

Finally, when we passed Barstow and got to San Bernardino we knew the end was in sight.

The roads in California suddenly seemed cleaner, wider, and smoother than anywhere else we had been. The interstate highway system was under construction then and California was leading the way.

We were making our way north through Southern California and still had a few hundred miles to go before we'd hit Monterey. But, once we got on the Pacific Coast Highway it didn't matter how long it took. We could see the vast Pacific Ocean and anything seemed possible.

Not sure what to say here, so make up your own caption!

CHAPTER FIVE

Monterey, CA

"There's a big difference between kneeling down and bending over."

~ **Frank Zappa**

With Maryland far in the rear view mirror we were seven days on the road. The closer we got to Monterey the more excitement buzzed around us.

Funny thing about spending time in the back seat of that Henry J—seeing palm trees, green and brown hillsides and the California style bungalow homes began to have a calming effect on Frank, Carl, and me.

We became less squirrelly and more alert as we drove through our soon to be adopted new state.

Mom, still holding Candy on her lap, mentioned to Dad that she was nervous about finding a new home. We'd never heard Mom question Dad about anything before.

Dad told her not to worry, that things would work out fine and soon we would all be glad we made the move.

Frank and I knew that leaving Mom's family behind in Baltimore was hard for her. It was not going to be easy for her nerves to get settled in a new home. Without ever saying anything to Mom we hoped Monterey might be the place that could help her worry less.

After passing San Bernardino, we drove through Los Angeles and headed north along the Pacific Coast Highway toward Monterey.

Monterey is a quaint seaside town on the central coast of California about 100 miles south of San Francisco and 300 miles north of Los Angeles.

The town overlooks Monterey Bay in the northern part of the Monterey Peninsula. Our first sight of Monterey relieved any anxieties that we'd had.

This first impression made the transition from the East Coast to the West Coast look hopeful.

We thought Dad might have been right. This move was beginning to look like a good idea.

Monterey isn't far from today's high-tech Silicon Valley and the California coastal region known as Big Sur.

The drive along Route 1, and the spectacular Pacific Coast Highway, convinced us that by leaving our old life behind, things would improve. Along this stretch of road we saw giant redwood trees and breathtaking turquoise blue ocean views.

This part of California was awe-inspiring and it made me think about things much bigger than myself. I fantasized about the good times to come.

It was never easy to read Frank while he stared out the window at the constantly changing landscape but he seemed to share my positive thoughts about this new life we were embarking on.

In 1951 Monterey was predominantly a middle class community. There were, of course, wealthy residents and a solid middle class driven by a commercial fishing industry. But Monterey was beginning to show signs of an economic slump.

We soon learned that the commercial fishing industry was on the decline and fishermen were losing jobs. The declining economy was offset by the area's natural beauty, which was a big tourist attraction.

Many prime real estate locations would soon bring an upturn in the region's housing market for those who recognized that growth potential.

Stocking Caps

In the short time that we lived in Monterey, Dad made time on the weekends to take us to historic spots and landmarks, especially Fisherman's Wharf. Initially, going on those family outings was great fun.

We got to see new sights and eat tacos and salty French fries. I loved those new tastes. As time passed I loved them too much. I wasn't built lanky like Frankie.

We watched other kids interact with their parents, which added to our excitement about being in a new place. Frank and I were participant observers, although we didn't know it at the time. You watch, you learn.

Mom's creative energy blossomed. She decided we should all have stocking caps when we went to Fisherman's Wharf. Nobody else was wearing stocking caps but that didn't deter our mom.

Handy with needle and thread, she crafted our caps out of old jerseys and attached little wool tassels that dangled from the top. They made us look like fugitive reindeer herdsmen or, in my case, an overfed elf.

We were required to wear them but we never fully understood her motherly logic that said wearing those stocking caps would help us fit in.

Frankie being silly, Bobby scratching his ass, Carl wearing his first leisure suit and Candy on her junior ride-around lawnmower.

The Portuguese fishermen, with gnarly hands and enormous knuckles wore caps with a brim, not the shapeless bags that our headgear turned out to be.

While Carl, Candy, and I didn't know any better about the stocking caps, Frank complained bitterly about having to wear his.

My brother was changing. He'd always been a keen observer of human behavior, but now he became much more vocal about what he viewed as the absurdities in life.

Frank was getting taller which made him look gawky and he seemed more self-conscious. He only agreed to wear his stocking cap when Dad threatened to quit taking us on outings.

Dad used strong-arm tactics by blaming Frank for screwing things up for everybody else. Frank usually knuckled under when Dad put him on notice like that but he bristled at the threats and resented Dad's ultimatums.

When Dad put Frank in that position, the outcome was never good. Frank was maturing fast and his challenges to Dad's authority were escalating. As for the caps, our father seemed to be motivated by a noble aim to support Mom and help her feel proud of this new handiwork hobby.

Dad told us to knock off the crap and stand at Parade-Rest.

But for Frank, wearing the stocking cap became a battle of wills.

Dad was unwilling to give up any control and when Frank rebelled, Dad pushed back even harder. The tension between Frank and Dad was growing worse. When Frank attempted to do things his way, Dad questioned his motives.

If Frank didn't provide a satisfactory explanation, Dad refused Frank. It seemed even worse when he'd let Frank do something, only to goad him into feeling bad about it afterwards.

One day Frank said, "I'd like to get a model airplane kit." Dad asked why. Frank said, "I've seen other kids building model airplanes." Dad said, "That's no reason. Who says you have to follow a crowd?"

I knew the real reason for not getting Frank the airplane kit was money. But instead of Dad simply telling Frank that he couldn't afford it, he put Frank on the defensive, implying that Frank was weak.

For my brother this was humiliating. It fed his resentments and strengthened his resolve to stand up to authority.

Family Portrait: Frankie playing pocket-pool, Bobby scratching his ass again, Carl doing the same, Dad being very proud and Mom and Candy wishing they were elsewhere.

Monterey and Portuguese Christmas

Monterey, California is home to the famous Naval Postgraduate School. There is also the Fleet Oceanography Center and the Defense Language Institute.

Dad's new job was at the Naval Post Graduate School. United States and foreign military personnel go to the NPGS to earn advanced degrees, including masters and PhDs.

Dad's job was to teach metallurgy, the properties of metals. He seemed excited about it.

The main focus of the Naval Postgraduate School is study and research programs for the Department of Defense. The campus had state-of-the-art laboratories, academic buildings, a library, government housing, and recreational facilities.

Most of the faculty was made up of civilian instructors from all sorts of educational backgrounds along with institutions representing an impressive group of scholars.

Dad's work at the Army Chemical Warfare Center in Edgewood, Maryland, qualified him for the position.

His teaching assignment was in Materials Science and Engineering where he taught courses in metallurgy as part of the Masters program. When dad wasn't teaching or preparing lessons at home he liked to go to Fisherman's Wharf.

We'd go as often as he thought we could afford to and if Mom felt up to it. She was less than enthusiastic about going, but she did enjoy seeing us wear our stocking caps.

Dad enjoyed walking around, taking in the ocean's crisp salt air as he watched people fishing off the pier. This family activity served as an escape from his daily grind.

Mom's reservations about going to the Wharf came down to money. We couldn't afford dinner for the six of us at any of the restaurants.

She would've loved to take us but the money Dad earned from teaching wasn't enough to live comfortably on. Mom wrestled with a tug of emotions, no doubt comparing our financial status to that of Aunt Mary and Uncle Robert.

In those early days in Monterey, Dad now seemed happier and more outgoing than he had been in Edgewood or Baltimore and certainly more than during our drive west.

He had regained some of his humor and enthusiasm. Living near the ocean seemed to have a calming effect on him. For that we were all grateful.

Dad took us to see old California missions. Walking through the grounds of those old churches we learned about the architectural monuments and religious history of the missions in the 1700s.

As usual, Frank was hungry with curiosity and asked questions that would never occur to the rest of us. Frank once asked the tour guide if the missionaries had wives back then.

The tour guide's eyebrows arched up in surprise. He was a priest, so chances are he was not used to questions like that, especially coming from a precocious 11-year-old boy.

The guide looked flustered, then he turned to my Dad and said, "My, my, what a curious young man."

After those field trips I always felt worldlier and reassured that Dad had made the right decision to bring us to California. That feeling of security didn't last long.

The first house Mom and Dad rented in Monterey was my favorite of the many homes we'd live in over the next few years.

It was an old two-story Victorian with a wrap-around porch and a big kitchen. It was an ideal place for me because I finally had enough room to let my imagination roam.

It was much bigger than our Edgewood house on the Army base and it made me feel better about myself. It seemed like we weren't so poor anymore.

Knowing the house was ours felt like we'd moved up in the ranks. I felt like we were important now and good enough to impress Aunt Mary.

At first it was hard for our family to make friends. Most of the other families in the area were not receptive to outsiders.

A few of the women were wives of Portuguese fisherman and tradesmen who had lived in the area for many years.

Theirs was a close-knit community but, after a couple of months, some of the neighborhood women began talking with Mom and she started to feel welcomed.

We began to receive invitations to dinner in their homes and Frank and I got to meet lots of kids. The Portuguese families we came to know were large:

sons, daughters, first cousins, second cousins, nephews, nieces, aunts and uncles.

Having left our relatives behind in Maryland, those large substitute-families helped make the transition easier.

There was also a sense of warmth and for a time we felt like we were on our way to becoming part of the fabric of this community. Frank wasn't as keen on belonging to a group.

He didn't make friends as easily as I did and he was sure we were never going to become part of their circle. His sixth sense proved to be right.

On our first Christmas in Monterey we were invited to dinner at the home of one of the Portuguese families.

The father was a successful fisherman with three boats and four grown sons who worked with him. Each of the sons had wives and children.

Together with the other family members, including the six of us, there were at least 30 people at dinner that night.

Their home was roomy and comfortable, with lots of holiday decorations including an enormous Christmas tree with more ornaments than I had ever seen.

At the base of the tree were dozens of brightly wrapped red and green Christmas presents. It was a tradition that each child was allowed to open one present after dinner. Mom and Dad looked as surprised as we were.

When it came time to open gifts, Frank, Carl, Candy, and I sat and watched wide-eyed as every one of the Portuguese kids was presented with a gift. Each child's face lit up when they pulled off the ribbons and tore open the paper.

I felt a huge letdown as those gifts were handed out. It was like shining a light on the fact that we were outsiders. We really did not fit in and I wanted to run out of the room.

I felt embarrassed, humiliated, and even guilty for the pangs of envy in my stomach. My cheeks burned with shame. It was the pivotal moment when Frank and I realized we would never be anything more than outsiders.

Candy and Carl may not have had the same awareness then but they would come to understand it better as our family continued to move from place to place.

Were the moves an attempt to find a better life, or were we just running away from who we were? That question was carved permanently into the back of my mind.

CHAPTER SIX

Pacific Grove

"I'm probably more famous for sitting on the toilet than for anything else that I do."

~ **Frank Zappa**

After living in Monterey for only eight months we moved to Pacific Grove. We left the big Victorian house we had come to love and the Portuguese families we were finally developing a connection with. We ended up in a smaller rental not far from the center of Pacific Grove.

None of us kids knew exactly why we had to move from Monterey, but Frank said it was about money, or our lack thereof. He said that must've been the driving force because it always was.

The sad, uncomfortable Christmas didn't help our spirits nor did the reality that we would never be able to reciprocate with dinner invitations.

So we had to say goodbye to Fisherman's Wharf and those wonderful weekend excursions. We left another school and the friends we'd just made. Frank and I talked about the weight of always having to start over.

On the plus side, our new home was closer to the downtown area of Pacific Grove and as Dad put it, we'd be starting in a new school and make new friends.

That became Dad's recurring pep talk. But the moves only intensified our stress and all we saw were bigger patches of loneliness growing fast and wild like moss. It pulled Frank and me tighter to each other, though.

It was a happy discovery when we first got to see the tidal pools along the Pacific Grove coastline.

Frank and I liked to run down to these cool tidal pools and wander around looking at the sea creatures living on the rocks and inside crevices. Once Dad went with us. He said he wanted to collect sea urchins.

We soon learned that sea urchins are edible and used in sushi. Dad told us that sea urchin roe is popular in Korean cuisine and that some people believe roe has healing powers.

Frank looked it up and explained to me that was because it contains a complex chemical compound that has been known to act as a bio-regulatory mechanism in treatments for medical conditions ... like I understood that.

Research had been done using sea urchin roe to treat arthritis, migraine headaches, anxiety, epileptic seizures, insomnia, loss of appetite, GERD (chronic heartburn), nausea, glaucoma, depression, bipolar disorder, multiple sclerosis, menstrual cramps, Parkinson's, trigeminal neuralgia (tic douloureux), high blood pressure, irritable bowel syndrome, and bladder incontinence.

A virtual pharmaceutical cornucopia contained in one tiny sea creature.And wouldn't you know those spiny little suckers were just lying around in the tidal pools waiting to be picked up.

All one had to do was fish one out to make a meal of it, which is exactly what Dad decided to do. He gathered up a few of the larger specimens and plopped them in a paper bag.

When we got home he set the bag on the kitchen table and took one out. He cracked it open with a large knife. The insides were orange and slimy mixed with little green globules.

Unfazed by its appearance, but curious to find out what it was like, Dad sliced a lemon in half, squeezed the juice on the contents, shook some salt on top, picked up the contents with a fork. Then he told me to eat it.

I was afraid to eat that little sea beast but here was my own father telling me to be adventurous and try something new, so how bad could it be? I ate the sea urchin and surprisingly it didn't taste half bad.

The texture felt disgusting though and I wretched. Dad interpreted that as a bad omen and put the rest of the sea urchins back in the bag and threw them in the trash.

Overnight the tossed sea beings stunk up the kitchen and I was left with the creepy feeling that he used me as the guinea pig in his little experiment.

3-D Movies and Looking Good

Pacific Grove was where Frank and I were finally allowed to do things on our own. The first time either of us went to the movies without an adult chaperone was in Pacific Grove. There was a new theater that had only been open a few weeks.

They were showing the movie "Bwana Devil" in 3-D. It was the first of many movies we would see together, but because it was our first movie by ourselves, and our first 3-D movie, this was special.

The night we went to the theater Mom made us wear a coat and tie. The absurdity of this cannot be minimized. Mom thought that going to the movies by ourselves meant that we had to look grown up.

Some of Aunt Mary's East Coast childrearing theories must have rubbed off on her but that one was woefully misplaced.

Dad drove us to the theater and let us out in front. He said he'd be back to pick us up right after the show.

Frank had money for the tickets and a little extra for candy and popcorn. When we got out of the car kids waiting to buy tickets saw us. They started laughing and pointing because of the way we were dressed. Frank said, "Just ignore them."

We got in line and I felt so embarrassed I wished I could disappear. It felt like wherever we went, we stood out. We were always the new kids, misfits who didn't dress right and got targeted with snickers and stares.

Frank and I responded differently to peer pressure. I fixated on food. I ate everything I could get my hands on. Frank went in another direction. He turned introspective.

As I continued to grow wider, he grew taller, leaner, and smarter. I accumulated calories; his anxieties burned calories off. He was growing handsome, aware, and confident. I on the other hand not so much.

By 1952, Frankie had grown four inches. The Northern California climate and a steady diet of fresh fruits and vegetables were exactly what he'd needed. Now 12, he was taller than most boys who were a year or two older.

He also developed an early maturity that was absent in his peers. I had grown too, but not up. I was a chunky lad with unruly hair and one furry eyebrow.

When mom bought me pants she'd buy them two sizes too long hoping that I'd grow into the length and not out of the waist. In order to wear those pants I had to turn up the cuffs, which made me look like a clown. Thankfully, Frank never made a big deal about how I looked.

He never made any cracks about my ridiculously huge pant-leg cuffs. He took care of me at the movie that night and so many more times while we were growing up. He was tolerant of my shortcomings, as I was of his. We were both deeply grateful that the other was there.

More Free Food

Pacific Grove isn't far from a place called Castroville, which, according to the Chamber of Commerce, is the "Artichoke Capital of the World."

Castroville sits in the heart of California's Central Coast farm country less than 100 miles from San Francisco and less than three miles from the Pacific Ocean.

It's also 10 miles from the town of Salinas in Monterey County, another big agricultural center in Northern California.

It was a marvelous place with the kind of countryside that did justice to the works of Jack London and John Steinbeck.

It wasn't yet the overpriced, over-developed, and over-populated haven for the rich that it later became. It had the luster of an idyllic rural environment that is now long gone.

On Saturday mornings in the summer, Dad packed Frank and me into the car. The three of us headed to the artichoke farms in Castroville.

It was Dad's belief that California, in general, and Castroville, in particular, were the land of the free.

By "free" he meant when no one was looking we could gather oranges, lemons, apples, plums, apricots, and cherries that were on the ground in the groves, as long as we were discreet. We were California's version of potato gleaners.

It never seemed to occur to Dad that this was thievery. Most of those fruits and vegetables were still edible and the growers would have had their workers gather them up to sell.

Dad felt entitled to helping himself and using us as fruit wranglers. He looked at it as his reward for working all week.

Artichokes, iceberg lettuce, and broccoli were what he considered prize catches so on those Saturday mornings we drove out to the large farms in Castroville, and Dad waited for the trucks headed to town to stop and deliver the crops for shipment.

Dad brought shopping bags on our morning scavenger hunts. We waited for the trucks to turn off of the dirt roads when they came from the fields and drove toward the highway. Artichokes bounced out when the truck tires made the jump from dirt to asphalt.

Dad turned Frank and me loose to grab the free artichokes. We picked up artichokes until we had two shopping bags filled with them. After that we went back to look for any other fallen vegetables.

Many of the artichokes we picked up off the street were just right for eating after the outer leaves were plucked off. Not so much with the iceberg lettuce. The heads of lettuce that fell off the trucks were pretty banged up.

We needed to collect three or four heads in order to salvage the equivalent of one head of lettuce. It would've been easier to purchase the lettuce at the market where we'd get it close to mint condition for only 15 cents.

Dad said the freebies we picked tasted better. At first, gathering fallen artichokes and lettuce seemed like the coolest thing we could do on a Saturday morning.

After a while, though, it began to sink in that we were doing this because we were poor. Dad was trying to make a game out of something that was, to him, a necessity.

Frank vented to me about the fact that we weren't able to do things other kids did or buy the same things they could. He became increasingly incensed about our financial situation.

He said, "One day I'm going to have enough money to do whatever the hell I want to." He sure was right about that.

During this period, Frank spent time concentrating on creative efforts. He finally got Dad to get him a model plane kit and was meticulous at putting it together.

He also constructed landscapes out of cardboard and made puppets out of paper mache, felt, wire, and pieces of cloth. This was the same time he developed a curiosity about explosives.

I remember Frank finding a cache of 50-caliber machine gun shells in an old garage in the neighborhood.

He said that he and a friend took some of those rounds and extracted the gunpowder from them to use in a rocket.

The tube was tightly packed with gunpowder. When he tamped down several caps for use in igniting the bomb, the caps went off prematurely and the gunpowder exploded. In the aftermath, Dad exploded more than Frank's bomb.

He shouted at Frank, "You stupid kid," and called him a "moron." He threatened to keep Frank grounded until he was 21. That, of course, didn't happen and it all blew over quickly, leaving Frank back on the street to wander off into more mischief.

Monarchs

Pacific Grove is a Monarch butterfly sanctuary. Every year in early October, hundreds of thousands of the little black and orange butterflies arrived at the end of their long trek from the Canadian Rockies and as far as southern Alaska.

Each year on a Saturday morning in October, Pacific Grove school kids dressed up like little Monarch butterflies and gathered at the edge of town.

The kids then paraded through the downtown section of Pacific Grove while parents and friends watched this annual ritual.

After the parade, there was a "Butterfly Bazaar" at the Robert Down School on Pine Avenue, which was the sponsor of the parade. This is where I went to school and where I participated in my first Monarch Day parade.

I had never done anything like that before and thought of it as an important event. I was anxious to make a Monarch butterfly costume and walk along with the other kids in their Monarch costumes.

We were instructed to begin making our costumes in school, and then finish them at home. Each kid had to show up at the parade in full Monarch butterfly attire.

I had no creative ability whatsoever and certainly no experience in butterfly costume design so I had an ominous premonition that mine would be the worst one in the parade.

The kids whose families had lived in Pacific Grove for a long time had their costume routine down pat and their plans looked stupendously elaborate.

Unfortunately, Mom and Dad weren't any help. Dad thought the parade was a nice thing for me but had zero interest in getting involved.

He was busy with work, budgetary challenges, and relaxing with his math puzzles in the evenings. He was most likely preoccupied with planning our next move and Mom's butterfly costume making skills were lacking, despite her previous talents at creating stocking caps.

Frank came to the rescue and helped me put my costume together.

He made wings out of paper mache and then attached black and orange crepe paper. With a black sweater and my new wings, I was a passable Monarch.

It was a small thing but it taught me I could depend on my brother when I needed him. Making a goofy costume may not seem like much, but when you need one and there is nobody else there to help, having my older brother help make butterfly wings made all the difference.

CHAPTER SEVEN

Claremont, CA

"My best advice to anyone who wants to raise a happy, mentally healthy child is: Keep him or her as far away from a church as you can."

~ **Frank Zappa**

In 1954, after living in Monterey and Pacific Grove for three years, Dad moved us to Southern California. I was 10 and Frank was 13 and neither of us was happy about leaving Northern California.

Dad said we were going to be better off elsewhere, so we packed up and headed south. Dad did get a better job. It was with Convair, a defense contractor in Pomona, California.

Convair specialized in developing and manufacturing land and ship surface-to-air missile systems, the Phalanx radar-controlled gun system, and anti-tank weapons.

Their specialty was making devices for killing people on a grand scale. It was a successful company and they paid Dad well enough for us to move into a nice tract home in Claremont, one of the tidy little college towns in Southern California, 35 miles east of Los Angeles.

Claremont is 60 miles inland from the Pacific Ocean and although Frank and I missed exploring the rocks and tidal pools in Monterey we were happy to be there. Claremont's village center had shops, offices, and restaurants bordering the seven Claremont Colleges.

Large Eucalyptus trees shaded the streets in the older residential areas. Another plus was that the town gave the impression of stability and permanence—something Frank and I were hungry for.

There were hundreds of acres of orange and lemon groves at the edge of town at the base of the foothills. Today most of those groves are housing developments. But in 1954, on cold winter mornings, orange grove owners sent workers to the fields to light smudge pots, oil-burning devices that were placed between rows of trees.

The pots were filthy black and each had a big, rounded bowl of a holding area where the smudging oil was poured in. Once lit, the pots gave off heat, and each had a smokestack with a hole at the top.

The heat and smoke generated by those fuel oil-burning pots helped keep the fruit from freezing. It also contributed to the growing problem of poor air quality in the valley. Breathing that air was almost as bad as the cigarettes Frank would soon be constantly smoking.

Another New School

Once we were settled there, Frank and I started at new schools, each only a short walk from home. Mine was El Roble on Mountain Avenue up the hill from Oak Park Drive, the street where our house was.

The best part about this school was that it was close by. We were the new kids on the block, again, and I felt intimidated. I was also academically disoriented from attending four different schools by age 10.

Getting to know teachers and classmates in one school and then having to move again created challenges for me. For one thing it was hard to keep names and places straight.

I scoped out each new scene in every new school and tried to figure out where and how to fit into the new environment.

Frank was older and more self-sufficient. He attended the junior high section of Claremont High School. He also used to visit a music store in Claremont called the Folk Music Center on Harvard Avenue.

The owners, Dorothy and Charles Chase, also opened the Golden Ring, a music cafe, one of the earliest venues for folk music in the Southern California area.

They brought such greats to Claremont as Brownie McGhee and Sonny Terry, Doc Watson, Hedy West, John Fahey, The New Lost City Ramblers, and Guy and Candy Carawan.

Frank would later become friends with Brownie and Sonny when we would go to the Ash Grove on Melrose Boulevard. His affinity for music and performing was growing exponentially during this period.

Meanwhile, preoccupied with finding my footing, I didn't focus on my studies as much as I should have. I watched a lot of TV. Our parents were distracted by their own issues and never pushed me to do well in school.

They never even checked to make sure I did my homework. Throughout my junior and senior high school years I had dysfunctional study habits born of apathy but being left alone to watch television was fine with me.

Frank didn't have trouble with schoolwork. He had good study habits and was always well prepared but only in subjects he liked. There is a psychological theory that musicians tend to be good at math. That was true in Frank's case.

As a band member in junior high he'd learned how to read music and gained an appreciation for orchestrated pieces.

He was also a voracious reader of things that interested him, especially science fiction.

Each morning we'd set out to school together. This lasted all through high school. We began carrying metal lunch boxes that Mom gave us at the beginning of the school year. The other kids all used paper bags. We were never in sync with our peers, which was a way of life for us.

After many years spent as outsiders, Frank had adapted by developing independence. Being part of the "in" crowd didn't matter to him. It took me longer but I, too, came to the same conclusion.

My decision-making process was usually a simple matter of following Frank's lead, something I had grown accustomed to over the years.

Amusements and Diversions

Dad seemed happy with this move. We knew he was making more money because we got to go on more outings as a family. Those were the days of Davy Crockett, the Mouseketeers, and Captain Kangaroo.

It was the beginning of make-believe as a main revenue source for big entertainment businesses in Southern California, a state of mind that dominated the culture in Los Angeles in the years that followed.

Dad loved all that escapism and expected us to enjoy it too. Unlike Fisherman's Wharf in Monterey, we didn't have to wear stocking caps when we went out. Mom also seemed happier in our new neighborhood.

It's possible that Mom had something to do with Dad's frequent job changes. He tried to please her by improving our family's lot in life.

But it's too bad we never stayed in one place long enough for her to watch us grow up in a stable environment or for her to participate with each of us during those formative years.

But if things had gone differently and if Frank's reactions weren't so extreme, he might never have turned out as unique, high-spirited, and prolific as he did.

At this time I was still wearing pants with enormous cuffs. My parents were still waiting in vain for me to have the same kind of growth spurt that Frank had.

Fortunately, his physical development in Claremont had not been hampered by his earlier medical treatments in Maryland, like the radioactive pellets one doctor inserted into Frank's nose to help with his asthma.

His pants always fit perfectly and maybe the pellet worked—Frank no longer wheezed like a bellows. My adolescent growth may have been delayed, but what I lacked in height I made up for in girth.

Dad continually tried moneymaking or money-saving schemes that didn't pan out. He was always looking for a solution. Once he purchased two milking goats that he kept in the garage at our house on Oak Park Drive.

His plan was to harvest the goats' milk daily. We'd be able to use it on our cereal and drink glasses of it in place of that pasteurized and homogenized cow's milk that was selling for a whopping 90 cents a quart in the supermarket.

It seemed like a workable plan until the neighbors complained about the smell and noise from our goats. During most of the day the goats were locked up in the garage eating hay and pooping on the garage floor.

An unventilated garage and the methane gas from goat shit was a disaster in the making. Minor details like these did nothing to deter Dad.

He was going to have free goat's milk, the neighbors be damned. As it turned out we never drank any of that milk. None of us knew how or even wanted to milk the goats, not even Dad.

A secondary plan he concocted was to sell goat manure as fertilizer, which never made it off the ground. There was no demand for goat manure.

For an educated man, Dad sure had a blind spot when it came to due diligence. None of us were interested in cleaning up the mess in the garage but Dad told Carl and me to do it. That was one nasty chore.

Dad saw himself as an entrepreneurial businessman. He was the only one who did, though.

The inevitable finally happened. One day, the village sent a policeman to the house. He was a polite older man who probably wondered about this peculiar family that was housing goats in their garage.

Frank and I came to the door when Mom answered his knock. At first I was afraid we were going to be carted off to jail.

Brave Frank stood there with Mom and when the policeman asked for Dad, Frank said, "Why?" The cop, looking at Frank as if he were in charge said, "It's illegal to keep goats in your garage or anywhere else within the city limits."

Just then, Dad came bustling in and muscled Frank, Mom, and me out of the way.

"What the hell is going on here?" Dad bellowed. The officer backed up a few steps and said, "I'm just the one picked to deliver the message."

The cop explained it was just a warning and there'd be no summons or ticket, this time. Dad calmed down. The cop left and Dad immediately turned on Frank.

"Mind your own damn business," said Dad. "What the hell do you know about dealing with the police?"

I saw on Frank's face that Dad's attitude stung and Frank walked out of the room. Dad then turned on Mom and said, "In the future, you are to come get me before you go speaking to any authority about things you obviously can't understand."

Dad finally sold the goats to a butcher. He used the remaining hay and goat droppings on the lawn in our backyard as payback to the neighbors who'd complained about the odor.

Sadly, the goat shit didn't do our lawn much good and our already shaky relationship with the neighbors became more tenuous as our lawn emanated a powerful barnyard aroma while simultaneously turning it brown.

Frank later told me that Dad could have purchased packages of inexpensive, odorless lawn chemicals at any hardware store.

Dad's next business scheme involved parakeets. He wasn't happy about having to give up his goats and was still determined to come up with a project using animals. His answer was to become a parakeet rancher.

Dad told us, "All you have to do is get a few parakeet boys and a few parakeet girls, let them hang out in the garage for a while and presto: more parakeets!

Then we'll sell them to the pet shops or you boys can set up a parakeet stand in front of our house and your mother will make the sign."

This first part of his plan took flight. The parakeets in our garage seemed to enjoy each other's company because soon we had little parakeets chirping up a cacophony. At one point we had 20 birds in the garage.

Alas, the new aviary did not sit well with the already agitated neighbors and constant chirping did little to appease them. While the goats had only occasionally let out baas, the parakeets couldn't contain themselves.

For a second time, the village sent a policeman to the Zappa ranch. Mom heard the knock and told me to go get Dad, which I did.

Dad came to the door and opened it with an aggressive yank and said to the cop, "Oh for Chrissakes, what is it this time?"

The young cop explained to Dad that neighbors had complained about the bird noises and odor and that keeping a large number of birds in the garage was not allowed. I wished he'd tell Dad to do something about his obsession with barnyard animals.

Now Dad had to come up with a strategic plan to unload a garage full of parakeets. He went into the garage to tend to his flock.

I guess he thought the birds needed some exercise. In his mind, that must've been where he'd gone wrong.

Dad thought he hadn't allowed them to move around enough. The logic was that if they were happier, they'd make less noise.

He opened the cage doors and the little creatures zipped out from behind the bars and began flying around the garage like angry houseflies.

Dad busied himself by sweeping up beneath the cages, and filling their feeders and water dishes. Mom came out to tell Dad he had a phone call. He left the garage by the side door and went into the house.

Before Dad went inside he told Carl and me to stay away from the garage.

He didn't think we were smart enough to keep the parakeets safe but we wanted nothing to do with them anyway and continued playing cowboys and Indians in the yard.

Dad came out of the house and went back into the garage. But, instead of going in the side door, he absentmindedly lifted the big garage door in front. The parakeets made a mass exodus out that door like speeding shotgun pellets.

With the exit strategy for birds now moot, and the garage mute, 20 happy parakeets took to the California sky. Thankfully, with the garage door open, the aroma issue was about to be resolved as well.

Our father's problem was that he was an "Old Italian" country boy at heart but a dreadful failure as a new world entrepreneur. He had all the drive but his ideas were tragically flawed.

Ghost Town

On weekends Dad occasionally took us to Knott's Berry Farm and Ghost Town in Buena Park, California. The Walter Knott family set out in the 1920s selling raspberries from a roadside stand.

By the 1930s, Walter Knott cultivated the world's first boysenberry, a combination of the red raspberry, blackberry, and loganberry.

By 1968 the Knott family recognized the business potential in their budding enterprise so they fenced in the buildings, opened a restaurant, and began charging admission to Knott's Berry Farm.

After its long successful history of hosting the first "Ghost Town," Knott's Berry Farm earned the title of "America's First Theme Park."

Ghost Town is the oldest part of the Knott's amusement park. It includes buildings brought to the property in the 1940s and 1950s. The narrow gauge Ghost Town & Calico Railroad, the Butterfield Stagecoach, and The Wild West Stunt Show, were Dad's favorites. Dad always got a kick out of seeing the bad guys get shot.

Frankie looking cool, Bobby with cuffs, Carl with an itch,
Candy praying, and Dad looking casual and the first photo
bomb (girl unidentified).

Our father was a big fan of TV westerns. Going
to Knott's was his fantasy come to life and he bought a
pair of cowboy boots.

Frank had a profound aversion to the life of the
cowboy, which made the re-enactment thing as boring
as watching hair grow.

Frank said the only good thing about those trips
was watching all the pretty girls. Frank would wander
off in the direction of a group of girls and Dad was
forever calling his name. The girl attraction was a big
factor in Frank's tolerance for Dad's constant
haranguing.

Frankie hoping to join the Italian Navy one day.

At home Dad used to sit in front of the TV in boxer shorts, athletic T-shirt, and a beret. Curiously, he never bought a western hat.

I was okay with Dad's eccentricities, as long he didn't wander outside looking like that. While Dad watched shoot 'em up westerns, he puzzled over math problems to relax. His problems always looked intense and very complex.

Frank made fun of Dad's bizarre behavior because that was his way of getting even with Dad's rigid rules and, frankly, because it was indeed bizarre.

But maybe Dad's math obsession had one good result: at their core, math and music both rely on counting and numbers.

Dad played guitar when he was in college and it may be that Frank inherited our father's obsession with math and possibly Dad's interest in music.

It's like both of their heads were always counting, calculating, and composing.

So, Frank got Dad's math gene and I was gifted with Dad's fat gene. It might have been that simple. No one in our family but Frank was tall and skinny.

The rest of us all had weight issues. Frank's metabolism was the opposite of the entire Zappa clan including our ancestors.

He could eat like a horse and not gain an ounce. I, on the other hand, needed only to walk past a bowl of pasta to go up a pants size.

It's interesting to think about the cards we are dealt at birth. Frank had health issues, like the asthma that plagued him as a child.

Yet he had the ability to see patterns and count rhythms and possessed an eclectic view of the music world that hadn't been witnessed since the days of the great composers.

Today there are courses still being taught about Frank's music at places like the University of North Texas and Indiana University. They take the students through an examination of the intricacies of "the American composer Frank Zappa."

Students study the originality of his music and the political, social, and cultural aspects of his trailblazing life. Not everybody can say something like that about their big brother.

The never-ending tension between Frank and Dad polarized their relationship. Frank's rage and resentment towards Dad about our constant upheaval, combined with their shared math gene, must've been the mixing bowl of combined ingredients that created the recipe for Frank Zappa, rock icon.

The Magical Kingdom

After a few visits to Knott's theme park Mom and Dad decided to step it up on nurturing our involvement with make-believe. All aboard, next stop Disneyland. Disneyland opened in 1955 in Anaheim, 26 miles south of our home in Claremont.

Originally it was planned as a private eight-acre park for Disney employees and their families on Riverside Drive next to Burbank, California. But early in the 1950s it became clear that the Company needed more land. They were planning a much larger park than the Burbank site could accommodate.

As successful as Disney was with their animated films, they had trouble obtaining enough funding to build a park on such a grand scale. Walt Disney decided to use television to plant the seed of Disneyland.

He created the television show, Disneyland, which was broadcast on the American Broadcasting Company (ABC) TV network. In return, the network agreed to help finance the new park.

A research study commissioned by the Disney Company suggested that there was a significant potential for the Disneyland amusement park. Based on this study, Disney bought 160 acres of orange groves and walnut trees in Anaheim for the future home of Disneyland.

That proved to be one of the most profitable investments Mr. Disney ever made.

Construction began on July 18, 1954 with a projected budget of $17 million. One year later, on July 18, Disneyland Amusement Park opened to the public. The day the park opened it was 110 degrees. A plumber's strike left water fountains dry and most of the toilets non-functional.

The asphalt, poured just the night before, was still soft. Ladies wearing high-heels found their heels sucked in and when they tried to walk, the sinking shoes were yanked off their feet.

Adding to the hot asphalt and drought, the restaurants and street vendors ran out of food. A gas leak shut down rides in Fantasyland, Adventureland, and Frontierland. All of these glitches notwithstanding, opening day of the park was a huge success.

We went to Disneyland that first day it opened. Frank had been anxious to see the park, because he knew there would be lots of shapely teenage girls running around. I was disappointed because we didn't get to go on all the rides.

There were so many people waiting in line we would have died of heat exhaustion or thirst before making it to the gate and most of the rides were more than our parents could afford.

The only ones we went on were the kiddie level rides, which I had to go on with Carl and Candy. Frank didn't want to join us because he was busy looking at girls.

Dad was always impatient due to a short attention span. His irritability was ruining the visit. He was a master of "approach-avoidance." Approach-avoidance refers to conflicts that occur when there is one goal that has both a positive and a negative outcome simultaneously.

While Dad really wanted to take us to Disneyland and let us have fun, he couldn't relax because he knew if we stayed too long we'd get stuck in traffic going home. His mind was always racing to the next thing leaving precious little time to appreciate the moment he was in.

We all became frustrated when he cut the great day short just to beat traffic. We didn't care about the downside of sitting in traffic as much as we enjoyed the upside of being at the park. Dad's impatience was especially difficult for Frank.

While the rest of us went along with Dad's agenda because we were too intimidated to say anything, Frank got to the point where he didn't want to go on family jaunts anymore because he was sick of being rushed.

For him it killed all the fun and turned these trips into stressful experiences. Dad couldn't stand Frank's "ungrateful" attitude and the two of them fought, which always upset the rest of the family, especially Mom.

Another fuse that lit arguments was when Frank wanted to go places with his classmates and Dad said, "Absolutely not."

Frank and Dad shouted at each other and Mom, who couldn't stand the contention, cried. Candy and Carl would run out of the room and I usually froze, filled with agida that I'd soothe later with food.

The fights between Frank and Dad could and would erupt at any time—when Dad came home from work, on a weekend morning, when Frank was eager to go out, or at dinnertime when a touchy subject like schoolwork came up.

Dad pointed his finger at Frank and wagged it at him to emphasize who was in charge. Dad's eyes became dark and scary and even though I wasn't directly in the line of fire, the tension made my jaw clamp.

When the shouting reached a piercing decibel Mom screeched at them to stop. Then she'd either burst into tears or run from the room.

Even with his advanced degrees and good intentions Dad was, in many ways, a tyrant. He saw himself as the dominant head of the household and whether he was right or wrong didn't matter. He lived by the old world Italian way.

He believed it was his job to be the patriarch and his right to demand respect from his wife and children.

In his mind, he was in charge so having his authority challenged by his oldest son was an unacceptable and disrespectful slap in the face. With more understanding and less machismo, things could have been different between the two of them and better for all of us.

Frank learned to control his rage. He recognized that life is unfair but also saw that the way one deals with that will determine one's fate. Instead of railing against the world, he was determined to change it.

His anger and frustration had a happy result, though. They drove him to an obsession with music and creativity.

We'd moved around too much and had limited social skills. Frank became a loner who internalized his feelings of disappointment and hostility. The more life felt unfair, the more he threw himself into a world of music and moral outrage.

After we settled in Claremont, Frank and I became more comfortable in our new hometown and we were able to make friends. For Frank, his interest in music became his connection.

He joined the orchestra in junior high playing drums. He participated in band performances and he got to know other students with similar interests in music.

I grew interested in sports and found myself running around and becoming more independent. I spent time walking into town and exploring places with boys my own age.

We played in the orange groves and the concrete aqueduct where we pretended we were in danger.

It was a relief to finally feel like part of a community and begin growing up.

That feeling wouldn't last much longer, though.

CHAPTER EIGHT

El Cajon, CA

"If you end up with a boring miserable life because you listened to your mom, your dad, your teacher, your priest, or some guy on television telling you how to do your shit, then you deserve it."

~   **Frank Zappa**

Dad came home one evening and announced that he'd landed a new job and we were moving. This was the last thing Frank and I wanted. Even Carl and Candy were old enough to understand what was happening and became upset about leaving.

Dad never offered us a choice. We began the relocation shuffle once again. The years of multiple moves affected each of us differently. Mom looked distraught and tired.

Frank exuded a combination of rage and resignation. Carl and Candy looked scared and my appetite increased.

The more Frank challenged Dad's heavy-handed authority, the more Dad asserted control.

During one ferocious argument at dinner Frank said it was wrong to make us keep moving. "You never let us stay anywhere," he shouted. "It's horrible being the new guy everywhere we go."

Dad yelled back, "When you can provide for a family, then you can make the decisions." Dad said, "As long as you live in my house, you better shut up and behave."

When they went at each other like that I was too afraid to interfere but always thought that Frank was right.

When the screaming of that fight died down, I went to Frank's room to tell him he was right. He was reading a magazine when I walked in but he didn't look at me.

I started to speak but he said, "Leave it alone, Bobby." I meant well but it was of little consolation.

Frank didn't seem to care what I thought and my attempts to make him feel better were ignored. Frank was becoming more self-reliant, confident in his own assessments, and didn't need my reassurances.

My own attitude toward authority was growing more resentful. All Frank and I wanted was a sense of belonging and stability in a community. Dad might have wanted that, too, but again his attitude fell under the heading of approach-avoidance. I think it's fair to say that Dad's main goal was to make more money so we could live a better life.

In spite of his old world attitudes and closed-mindedness, he wasn't a monster. He was just a guy trying to provide for a family of six but everything he tried to do failed and he had no skills to talk about his feelings or ours.

He didn't have many friends because he didn't know how to bond. I think he filled his head with math to avoid feeling like a failure. His self-esteem must've been in the toilet.

And Frank, who was always getting emotionally beat up by Dad, distanced himself from his feelings of failure by filling all of his thoughts with music.

Meanwhile, Dad was becoming the poster boy for the military-industrial complex employee who jumped at every chance to relocate at any moment's notice. We never knew the specifics of why it was necessary for us to keep moving so often.

Dad told us it was for a better job or a better house or a nicer town. When things never worked out the way Dad had said they would, he never explained the failures and never apologized for his screwball ideas. In his head, he was the man of the household therefore he owed us no explanation.

The relocations taught me some important skills about people, like how to size them up, mimic them, and make friends with them.

If I could figure out how other people survived then maybe I could survive, too.

This lifestyle taught me a level of tolerance and the need to be resourceful in my survival skills. Later, when in the Marines, I was better prepared for the rapid deployments we were forced to endure.

The same upbringing affected Frank differently. He channeled his learning energies into succeeding at any cost.

After a year of living in Claremont we packed up and moved farther south to El Cajon, a town east of San Diego. Dad said it would be a good move because we'd be closer to the ocean again.

That turned out to be false because El Cajon is 15 miles inland and nowhere near the ocean.

We went from our comfortable house in Claremont on Oak Park Drive to a well-used rental house in a nondescript neighborhood. We were all disappointed in this move but too afraid of Dad's temper to complain loud enough for him to hear.

In the mid-to late 1950s, El Cajon was mainly a farming community. There were large vegetable farms and fruit orchards owned by farmers who used migrant labor from across the border in Mexico to work their crops.

Today El Cajon is part of the typical California suburban sprawl with strip malls, car dealerships, and fast food outlets. In 1955, El Cajon had a population of about 55,000.

It was predominantly White, with a quarter of the population made up of African Americans, Native Americans, Asians, Pacific Islanders, Hispanics, and Latinos.

El Cajon was a rough place to live. As with all our other moves, we moved there to be closer to Dad's new job, wherever the hell it was this time. We'd stopped asking and he'd stopped talking about what he was doing.

Frank started the ninth grade at Grossmont High in El Cajon. By then he was 5' 6" and scrawny-thin with no athleticism. His hair was greasy and he was plagued by teenage acne.

He had already been smoking for quite a while at that point but didn't drink. He had little interest in academics but quite a bit in music and art.

Frank began experimenting with watercolors, oils and charcoal, listening to jazz, blues, rock and roll, and classical music. He was on a learning curve that had little to do with the classroom.

One triumph for him was the prize he won for a poster he designed for the San Diego Fire Prevention Week contest.

In the picture that appeared in the local paper with him holding the poster, he looked pleased with himself because one of his talents had been duly noted. I think that gave him a boost in confidence and made him feel good about pursuing creative avenues.

In El Cajon Frank met Junior Madeo, the leader of the Ramblers rock and roll band. Junior's only connection to fame later on was being remembered as the guy who fired Frank from his first band for "riding the cymbals too much."

Frank begged our parents to buy him a real drum set and they finally agreed. The kit was fifty dollars, which was a lot of money back then. He hadn't yet become much of a drummer but he had big hopes and lots of ambition.

His problem was coordinating his foot on the bass drum while handling the drumsticks. It was clear to me the drums were not his instrument, and I wasn't surprised when Junior Madeo fired him.

When that happened Frank was disappointed but resilient. He didn't close up and feel sorry for himself. He took that rejection in stride and moved on to the next thing.

Frank's time with the Ramblers was not wasted. Frank learned from Junior's rejection. The experience helped him focus more on his growing fascination with music.

He realized quickly that he had much more talent than most of the guys he was playing with.

He got better and from that point on took control of the music. He played what he wanted to play and who he wanted to play it with.

CHAPTER NINE

Clairemont, CA

"Children are naïve -- they trust everyone. School is bad enough, but, if you put a child anywhere in the vicinity of a church, you're asking for trouble."

~ Frank Zappa

After a year in El Cajon we moved again. This time we didn't move far, just a little farther northwest to a small town called Clairemont—not to be confused with Claremont near Pomona.

Clairemont sat on a hill overlooking Mission Bay. From spots in our new neighborhood we could even see Mission Bay and that was a tiny plus.

The nice, albeit spotty view did little to offset this move, though. El Cajon had not been a great place to live but at least we'd had a larger house there. In

Clairemont, we'd traded that in for a small duplex apartment.

It was one more disappointment in a chain of downward spirals from our relocation shuffles.

By this point Frank and I were resigned to the upheaval in our lives. Frank channeled his energies into music, art, and expanding his understanding of the way people lived.

He was always curious and acutely observant, which aided him in formulating his views of the world.

One bright spot in Clairemont was the nearby University of San Diego, a Catholic college set on 180 acres overlooking Mission Bay. The buildings were Spanish-inspired and the grounds meticulously maintained.

It's still one of the more scenic private campuses in Southern California. It gave me a sense of hope to live near a university. It made me think I might be able to go to college one day. I imagined getting a job mowing the lawn there.

When I told Frank he made fun of me and said, "Aim higher." That was his way of smacking me on the back of the head but with words.

After we got settled Mom found the Catholic Church of the Immaculate Conception, located right down the hill from our duplex. Frank and I would go with Mom, Carl, and Candy on Sundays.

Even though we were falling away from the church, at least it was something to do and it was closer to Mission Bay, where we liked seeing the beach and the small amusement park located nearby.

After mass one Sunday, I dashed out the front door and ran smack into a priest. I was bigger by then and not overly coordinated so I gave him a jolt but he didn't go down.

What he did do was grab my shirt, smack me on the back of the head, and yell, "Stop running, boy." Frank came out of church at that moment and saw the priest hit me.

Always my protector, Frank went right up to the priest and said, "Keep your hands off my brother." I held my breath.

It looked like the priest was about to haul off and punch Frank. Just then Mom came out with Carl and Candy.

Realizing something was wrong, she asked the priest what happened. When he asked her if we were her children, she nodded. He said, "How long have you been parishioners here?"

"We've only just moved in," Mom said. "We're right up the hill in Clairemont." The "spiritual" leader said to Mom, "Surely you can find a church closer to home." With that he turned and walked away.

The incident was chilling and only confirmed Frank's and my own disdain for organized religion.

Mom & Dad – Close, but not touching.

Get a Job. Go to work. Be a jerk.

For the most part, life in Clairemont got better the longer we lived there. We were in a nice neighborhood, the weather was sunny and mild, and I was able to make a few friends at school.

One boy I got to know in my sixth grade class was a Mexican lad named Roy; he was a wild child with a wicked sense of humor.

One day in class he wouldn't stop talking so the teacher, an older woman who spent most of her time sitting in a chair in front of the class, yelled at Roy to be quiet or she would send him to the principal.

That shut him up for a few minutes but I guess the teacher could tell he was restless and needed a diversion.

She instructed him to go to the classroom blackboard. Roy got up from his seat and just as he was walking behind the teacher's chair he stopped and on command farted on her shoulder.

The room erupted into hysterical laughter as the teacher jumped up, grabbed Roy by the arm, and hustled him out of the room to the principal's office. Moments like that I remember fondly. Laughing was always such a great stress reliever.

I got my first real job, a paper route delivering the weekend San Diego Union Tribune. I delivered the Saturday and Sunday newspapers on foot because I didn't have a bike.

Around my neck hung a double-sided saddlebag stuffed with the papers.

As I walked my route, I'd throw the Tribune on my customers' front lawns. I was pretty good at it because it only required a little muscle and no heavy thinking.

It gave me a rush to be making my own money and, after a few weeks, I had earned enough to purchase my first 10-speed bicycle with Mom and Dad's financial help. Suddenly delivering the papers got a whole lot easier.

Another nifty perk of having the bike was that it allowed me freedom to go places with my friends. I kept it clean and watched the air in the tires and I always parked it carefully in our garage so as not to scratch it. I treasured it.

One Sunday morning while delivering newspapers, as I crossed an intersection in the crosswalk, an elderly lady driving a Buick screeched around the corner and hit me.

I flew off my bike and newspapers sailed out of the saddlebag. The Buick ran over my bike and mangled it beyond repair. I was knocked unconscious and rushed to the hospital.

When I came to, Mom and Dad were next to the bed. I heard them ask the doctor if I might have permanent brain damage. I hadn't been wearing a helmet when I hit the pavement. The doctor said he didn't think so.

When I was knocked off my bike I landed on my saddlebag, which broke the fall and prevented any serious cracks to my head.

As I was stretched out on the bed I began to worry that my dispatcher was going to be mad when he found out I didn't deliver the papers, which turned out to be the case.

Mom told me the next day that the policeman who'd called the ambulance said the accident was my fault for not watching the traffic when I crossed the street.

The cop told my parents that the woman who hit me had damaged her car but she was not going to press any charges. He told my parents they could ask the woman to buy me a new bike.

They asked. She refused. I lost my job as a paperboy along with my new bike.

Frank said that the old lady was in the wrong but that she probably knew the cop or had been in the neighborhood much longer than we had so she had the law on her side.

He also said that I had to be a lot more careful, which was a firm grasp of the obvious, but it was his way of trying to show concern and trying to help lessen the blow of losing my bike, my job, and almost my life.

Frank was now in tenth grade attending Mission Bay High School on Grand Avenue in San Diego. Mission Bay High was a tough place. It was filled with pachukos, Mexican gangs who fought with white kids and the other pachuko gangs.

The pachukos were the next generation after the Zoot Suiters in California. They took great pride in their gang uniforms that consisted of starched khaki work pants, long-sleeve shirts buttoned all the way to the neck, and spit-shined French-toed shoes with razor blades stuck in the sole at the toe. If you got kicked with the razor-toed shoe the damage was severe.

Frank kept a low profile at Mission Bay because the threat of violence was always in the air. He couldn't hang out after school. That was when the pachukos did most of their head banging. Frank kept to himself to avoid the gangs.

As a result, he had very few friends at Mission Bay High. During this period of his life he got more and more into 1950s rock and roll but even that didn't cheer him out of this new low ebb in his life.

Finally he made a few friends in the neighborhood. In his autobiography he tells the story about an experiment he and his friends did with mason jars. They peed in the jars and left them on a shelf in a garage at one boy's house.

After a few weeks they noticed little black things swimming in the urine, that Frank named "urine wogs." His fascination with so many peculiar things always amazed and amused me.

After my accident I felt sorry for myself. Life wasn't fair and I was very angry that my bike had been destroyed and that I'd lost my job.

Restless and angry, I got in with a crowd of crazy guys. One was a boy nicknamed Jack who had a talent for breaking and entering.

One night I went with him and two other boys to the strip mall near our apartment complex. It was 10:30 p.m. and all of the stores were closed.

We wandered around the mall buildings until we came to the back of a sporting goods store that sold rifles, handguns, ammunition, and sporting equipment.

Jack saw that one of the windows at the sporting goods store was open, so he motioned me and the other guys over to boost him up so he could climb in.

He was inside for about 10 minutes. When he came back to the window he handed us two .22-caliber bolt-action rifles and a box of .22 shells. We took the rifles and ran down into the ravine behind the mall.

Jack showed us how to load the rifles and we spent an hour shooting randomly in the dark. We were down in a gully behind the mall and away from the road so the noise wasn't loud enough to attract attention.

When we'd used up the ammo, we casually walked back to the store. Jack climbed back in the window. We handed him the rifles and he put them back in their racks.

He climbed back out and we all walked home. I thought about how easy and fun it was to break federal, state, and local laws and nobody was any the wiser.

When I went home and bragged to Frank about how we'd gotten away with it, I was laughing.

All of my pride and excitement quickly evaporated when Frank said, "You're an idiot and lucky you didn't get caught. You could've gotten in deep shit for that." When he saw how deflated I looked, Frank patted me on the shoulder and said, "It's good you got out there and had some fun."

That made me feel a little better but just as I was about to smile he said, "Just don't ever do anything that stupid again."

I'll forever be grateful, though. Frank was the only one looking out for me, teaching me how to get along in the world. At times like that he was like a parent, the helpful kind that explained things.

Frozen Assets and Time to Go

When Dad wasn't looking for a new job or free food, he was on the alert for bargain deals, and found one when he signed a contract with a wholesale meatpacking company in San Diego.

The company offered a free freezer for the term of the contract if you paid for a monthly purchase of certain cuts of meat and spent a specified dollar amount.

Dad said this was great because we'd be able to eat as much meat as we wanted and the freezer was free.

The lid on the freezer opened up like a coffin. Dad told the delivery guys to put it in the kitchen. Our kitchen wasn't big enough to comfortably house the monstrous freezer; it took up a third of the room. The good news was we had plenty of frozen meat.

We'd lived in Clairemont for almost a year when Dad came home one evening and announced, "We're moving." This time we were heading up to Lancaster, California in the Mojave Desert.

He told us he had landed a job working on a defense project at Edwards Air Force base in Palmdale, the town next to Lancaster.

If he'd had the slightest bit of sensitivity he would've seen the heartbroken stare in our eyes. But his excitement overshadowed everything. He was like a racetrack bettor, always sure this time would be the windfall. We all nodded and went back to what we'd been doing.

While we were packing up again, Dad told the meatpackers we no longer needed the freezer or the meat. They informed him they'd be happy to pick up the freezer but he was still under contract to pay for the meat. Another "great bargain" that cost us a lot of money.

Parting Shots

As we neared the end of our days in Clairemont, rough neighborhood kids were hassling Frank and me. We were now viewed as transients who needed to hurry up and get out.

One night after dinner, Frank and I were in the garage in back of the duplex sorting things into boxes. Three guys came walking by and stopped to taunt us, "Get the hell out, wetbacks. Nobody wants you here." One guy looked at me and said, "Get your ass back to Tijuana, fat boy."

Frank told them to fuck off which gave me a boost of confidence and I yelled, "Yeah, get the fuck out of here." One of the boys came toward me and punched me hard in the shoulder.

I longed for that croquet mallet I'd used on Frank's head in Baltimore but I improvised with what I had, an empty plastic squirt gun.

I smashed it onto the nose of the boy who'd hit me. The plastic cracked right along with his nose. Then the real fighting began. Next thing I knew Frank and I were getting pummeled by two of the guys. The kid I'd hit in the face just stood there screaming as blood gushed from his nose.

I lost it. Years of frustration turned into rage-filled adrenaline and I bent forward like a football player. I charged and rammed my head into the stomach of the guy hitting me.

I pushed him out of the garage and into the alley where he fell to the ground. I turned my attention to the guy who was beating up on Frank.

I grabbed his shirt and pulled him off my brother and then I punched him hard behind his right ear. It felt good, so I punched him again, this time on his neck.

He staggered back then tried to come at me, but I rushed him first. Bam! Down he went. The other kid tried to get up but Frank pushed him down again. The bleeding nose guy threatened us, "You're gonna pay for this, you fuckers."

As they walked away, one suddenly bent over, picked up a rock and threw it. It hit the garage. I grabbed a bigger rock and hit one of them in the thigh.

"You're dead meat, motherfuckers," the guy I hit in the thigh screamed. Fortunately, we never saw them again. The thing is, Frank and I never wanted to fight anybody.

We didn't feel good about it. But the way we'd teamed up and defended ourselves served as a reminder of how much we relied on each other.

Soon after that our family packed up, left Clairemont, and headed for Lancaster. Our experiences in San Diego left me with the unshakable feeling that no matter what I did, trouble was always just around the bend, waiting to pounce.

It also occurred to me that Frank wasn't always going to be on hand when it hit. That scared me but also made me know that, while it lasted, my big brother and I were a pretty good team—Batman and Robin, The Lone Ranger and Tonto, Frankie and Bobby.

Our route from Clairemont to Lancaster took us past La Jolla, San Clemente, San Juan Capistrano, and Laguna Beach. This was the trip where we said goodbye to cool sea breezes and ocean sunsets and hello to the sweltering, cactus infested Mojave Desert.

We passed through Newport Beach and drove northeast toward San Bernardino. We continued farther north toward Palmdale and Lancaster, having no idea what was ahead.

CHAPTER TEN

Lancaster, CA

"There is no such thing as a dirty word. Nor is there a word so powerful that it's going to send the listener to the lake of fire upon hearing it."

~ **Frank Zappa**

Dad's new job was with an aerospace company located at Edwards Air Force Base in Palmdale, north of Lancaster. Although he had his faults, Dad deserves credit for earnestly trying to improve our quality of life.

By now we'd moved from Baltimore to Monterey to Pacific Grove. From there we moved south to Claremont then we'd packed up and traipsed farther south to San Diego—El Cajon first, then Clairemont. Finally we'd gone north and landed in Lancaster. It had been just five years since we'd left Baltimore in the Henry J.

Our sister Candy, now six, was adaptable and still very close to Mom. The two of them drew strength from each other.

Carl did his best to keep up with the changes but he became overwhelmed and withdrew. As tough as the moves were, Frank seemed to adjust with the least visible trauma.

To blunt his feelings of frustration he read voraciously and soaked in as much knowledge as he could. He studied places we'd been and things we'd done to understand what he thought, who he was, and where he was going.

His alpha-dog leadership skills had first sprouted and now they were blooming.

I had acquired and honed different skills to help me make friends. By then I didn't much care where we lived as long as we had TV, enough to eat, and things to do. I still was optimistic about the future, but learned to live a day at a time.

I wasn't concerned about grades and never felt competitive with other students because so many of our moves occurred in the middle of a school year.

I felt out of place and was always behind other students in the content of the courses I was supposed to be taking.

How Hot Was It?

The Mojave Desert gets on average less than six inches of rain a year. By contrast, the average amount of rainfall in New York City is 45.5 inches annually. The Mojave is home to the hottest place in North America: Death Valley. The temperature there regularly approaches 120 degrees in late July and early August.

In spite of the blistering heat and lack of moisture, the Mojave, and especially its Antelope Valley, has long been California's center for alfalfa production.

The alfalfa fields are fed by irrigation from groundwater and the California Aqueduct. Many of our high school classmates lived and worked on alfalfa farms.

As hot as it gets in the summer, the Mojave can turn bitterly cold in winter going down to zero degrees.

Much of the Mojave typically ranges from highs over 100 degrees in the summer to lows of an average 20 degrees in the winter.

This time Dad had given us some of the details about his new job ahead of time. He'd elaborated on how exciting it would be to live in the high desert.

By then we'd grown weary of his enthusiastic yet off-kilter predictions and tuned him out. Frank and I had attended nine different schools by then. I was in ninth grade and Frank was a senior.

Desert Eclectic

When we got to Lancaster I immediately hated the town and its monotonous desert landscape. I detested the oppressive heat and small town mentality. I missed eucalyptus trees.

I missed being near the ocean. I hated the flatlands. For me Lancaster was like burning up in Hell. Settling in was not going to be easy.

Our first home there was another duplex close to the center of town. We lived in that duplex for a year until Dad figured out that we could afford a brand new house in a development on the edge of town that was close to the high school. The address was 45438 Third Street.

It was a four-bedroom chicken wire and stucco California ranch home built on a cement slab with a two-car garage. Being in our first new home helped ease the pain of being stuck out in the desert—but not much.

The housing development was devoid of trees and since the homes had been hastily constructed there were still piles of scrap lumber, cinderblocks, dried stucco lumps, shards of wallboard, twisted metal scraps, and other construction detritus on the front lawns.

The workmanship inside the house was shoddy and the fixtures and appliances were of poor quality. Those drawbacks notwithstanding, it was a new house and that meant a great deal to Mom.

There was no grass anywhere because the housing development sat literally on the edge of the Mojave Desert.

The summer temperatures in Lancaster soared to 105 degrees or more by midday. Grass never stood a chance.

Each home in the development had to have central air-conditioning because without it life would have been unlivable.

After we moved in, Mom and Dad began furnishing the house with what is best described as "desert eclectic." They bought a collection of chairs, sofas, end tables, lamps, and carpets, none of which matched or blended into any kind of interior design.

We did, however, have a state-of-the-art television, which became the center of our family's existence. This was true for many other families in that hot, miserable town.

Dad was so completely fixated on TV that he decided it was going to be our main source of amusement to the exclusion of just about any other family activity.

There were no more excursions, no more Disneyland, or Knott's Berry Farm. At first the rise of the TV and the demise of our family outings didn't bother me that much.

Frank and I found that we could easily make friends with kids of any economic and ethnic backgrounds if we used the common ground of TV shows, like American Bandstand.

Music was the common denominator back then and something we could all talk about. As we began making a few friends with neighborhood kids, their parents sometimes invited us to go along on outings.

They even seemed happy to include us so I couldn't just sit around sulking over our transient home life.

One kid Frank and I spent a lot of time with was Randy DeWeese. Randy's father built a bowling alley in Lancaster and we spent many happy hours there bowling for free and hanging out having fun.

Although Randy was my age he and Frank got along well. We also got to know Randy's father and he was the first adult we'd ever met who owned a business. We were impressed.

Randy's dad saw me in the same way that he saw his own son: a shy, awkward, pimply-faced adolescent. Frank, on the other hand, quickly developed an intellectual connection with Randy's father.

Although Frank was still a teenager he became intrigued with running a business and asked tons of questions about what it took to run the bowling alley. Randy's father seemed pleased by Frank's interest and happy to talk about it.

Frank was able to communicate well with a diverse collection of people. I, on the other hand, was still working my way through acne, weight, and raging hormones. Frank was evolving into an articulate, thoughtful, and curious person; I was still pudgy, horny, and a lousy bowler.

Our similarities were decreasing but our bond stayed as strong as ever. You couldn't spend time with one brother without the other. Frankie and Bobby were the dynamic duo.

High School Nightmares

It didn't take long for us to be reminded that no matter where we lived we were never part of the mainstream.

Antelope Valley Joint Union High School in Lancaster (AVJUHS) proved to be as unwelcoming as all of the other places.

Frank was in his senior year and he had a mix of courses and credits from the previous schools he'd attended. I was a freshman in a vocational program.

We weren't part of any social groups there, nor would we ever be. We were viewed as "ethnic" by members of the farming community. Lancaster was a white bread and bottled milk town. If you weren't like them you didn't belong in the herd.

It didn't help that Frank and I didn't know the rules for organized sports. Moving around as much as we did wasn't conducive to accumulating that kind of knowledge and experience.

Frank never wanted to play sports; it wasn't his thing. I would've been interested in them if I hadn't felt so intimidated by my lack of experience.

There was talk, mostly from Dad, about college for Frank. I had never once thought of my brother as college material.

He was smart enough, that's for sure, but the things he wanted to do didn't include spending four more years in a classroom.

Back then in the late 1950s Lancaster was a small town struggling to get away from its farming roots. The center of town had a few restaurants, a movie theater, various shops, and a grocery store.

But the alfalfa farms, sheep and cattle ranches, and vegetable farms scattered throughout the area were the dominant source of employment.

The students who lived on those farms and ranches usually did chores before they came to school. They had a strong work ethic but their options were limited because the local high school placed little emphasis on college.

The school's core mission was more about how to be on time for class and complete what you were asked to do.

Intellectual development was not high on the list of importance; it was far overshadowed by an emphasis on learning practical skills, like typing and building a shadow box in woodshop.

All seniors were encouraged to get a high school diploma, but there was no organized effort towards college admissions.

As it turned out Frank didn't have enough credits to graduate but the administration let him go anyway. Perhaps they didn't want him hanging around another year.

He wasn't what you'd call an easy student. His personality was too strong for that. He was cynical and argumentative. He was also creative and innovative and except for a few of the teachers, he was a lot sharper than them.

During the '50s, teenagers shared a passion for rock and roll. It was the era of Richie Valens, the Big Bopper, and the Penguins. It was the time of Jan and Dean and the Beach Boys.

It was also when Frank formed his first band, the Blackouts. This band changed the course of his life forever. The Blackouts had the best mix of teenage musical misfits Lancaster had ever seen.

There were African Americans, Mexicans, and rednecks. Wayne Lyles played percussion and sang vocals. Carter Franklin was also a singer.

Terry Wimberly played piano and Wally Salazar was on guitar. Fred Salazar, Wally's brother, and

Ernie Thompson played trumpet along with Steve Wolfe, Dwight Bement, and Johnny Franklin on sax.

Jim Sherwood played sax, danced, belched and had the best attitude of any of the band members. I think he had finally found his niche in life and was having a ball.

Frank played drums, but found it increasingly difficult to direct the group from behind the set, so he decided to switch to guitar so he could lead from the stage front.

Most of the African American band members lived on the outskirts of town in an area called Sun Village, Lancaster's version of a black ghetto.

Frank and I spent many great Saturday and Sunday evenings there with band members and their families playing music, eating fried chicken, and drinking cheap beer or peppermint schnapps.

I got to know a few other residents of Sun Village who would come and listen to the rehearsals. One of them was an older guy who was always loaded. In a moment of adult judgment gone haywire, he gave me a switchblade knife.

While I was partying with the locals and building my own cache of weaponry, Frank was perfecting his skills as a conductor, performer and orchestrator.

He, too, had found his niche. With The Blackouts Frank knew what he wanted—exactly how each note should be played, how long the songs should last, and the correct sequence for solos.

The trouble was the band members didn't always follow his lead. The musicians kept trying to do things their way instead of his. Frank couldn't stand it when he knew something would be better his way and others didn't comply.

Frank was strong-willed and intense and was developing an air of leadership. His need to control was in the burgeoning phase and needed a lot of finessing.

The Blackouts band brought about one of Frank's many learning spurts. He was learning how to manage people, organize things the way he wanted them, and develop a system to evaluate the musical abilities of performers who wanted to play in his band.

Captain Beefheart

During this time, Frank and I met Don Vliet. Don was from Glendale, California and his family moved to Lancaster in 1958 at around the same time we did.

Although a bit introverted, Don had an uncanny ability to imitate dialects, mimic different blues musicians, and create the oddest noises.

Don's vocal abilities would set Frank and me into fits of laughter as he imitated the guttural sounds of a blues singer, the high-pitched squeal of a back-up singer or a variety of barnyard animals. His vocal versatility cannot be minimized. He was a one-man cartoon symphony.

Frank and Don made up hilarious parodies of popular songs. Together they wrote the script for a movie they called "Captain Beefheart and the Grunt People." Don would later adopt "Captain Beefheart" as his stage name.

Befriending Don helped us cope a lot better with life in the desert. He was not as bitter as we were about living there and he inspired us with his constant chatter of places he was going to go and things he couldn't wait to do as soon as he escaped from high school.

Frank, Don, and I spent hours listening to rhythm and blues records and talking about how limited our lives were. A universal problem for outsiders like us was the missing girlfriend factor.

It was hard for Frank, Don, and especially me, to meet girls who didn't mind being seen with unpopular misfits like us.

Most of the cute girls wanted to hook up with local farm boys who drove pickup trucks, wore manly boots, had packs of cigarettes wrapped up in the sleeves of their T-shirts, and looked like nobody would mess with them.

Skinny, weird Frankie, daydreamer Don, and awkward, pudgy Bobby didn't stand a chance of getting noticed, let alone laid.

Frank and Don shared a similar sense of humor about their deep distrust of the establishment.

They also both smoked Winstons. Because Don looked older he could buy us beer, usually Brew 102, a local diarrhea-producing beverage, which we would secretly drink in his room while his parents were watching TV.

Frank wasn't as keen on the beer as I was but he did love toking up those cigarettes. It wasn't long before Don began spending time with us in Sun Village with the band members.

His own interest in music was deepening and it felt great to have him around. Hanging around with Don made us feel halfway normal.

Meet Mr. Tool Box

Our time in Lancaster drifted between upbeat times with friends like Don and the musicians in Sun Village to what happened to me in my freshman year.

During a woodshop class, a few of the rowdy students got revved up and began throwing screwdrivers, levels, and nails.

I wasn't participating because it seemed childish and idiotic. I also had the sense to know that horsing around near sharp grinding tools and a lathe was dangerous.

The shop teacher was a strange and solitary man named Mr. Bonner.

His typical outfit was a blue bowtie with a short sleeve button up white shirt under his shop tunic. He was too meek to be a take-charge kind of instructor and his workshop skills were lacking.

He fumbled around and sweated easily and profusely. He muttered at a really low pitch so you'd have to lean in to hear him and none of us wanted to bother so we mostly ignored him.

His peculiarities and inability to relate to us ninth graders left him clearly out of his depth as a teacher.

We nicknamed him Mr. Tool Box but behind his back he was always Mr. Boner.

As the tools and nails flew and chairs toppled over, Mr. Bonner couldn't get control of the class. The bell rang and the troublemaking kids ran out of the shop, abandoning their jobs to clean up their workstations.

I had been working near those kids and was cleaning up my area when suddenly Mr. Bonner charged at me, grabbed my arms, and pinned me backwards across the workbench.

Leaning over me with his horn-rimmed glasses almost pressing against my nose, he started yelling, "You little shithead! Can't you see I'm trying to teach a class in here? You think that's funny?" I was frozen in his grasp and too shocked to know how to react.

I was really frightened and had no idea what he was going to do next. All I knew was that I was pinned and his grip was hurting my arms.

Meanwhile, the students who had remained in the classroom were also frozen, like standing sculptures, as they watched Bonner holding me over the bench. I'm lucky I didn't wet my pants; I never would've lived that down.

Suddenly, as if abruptly changing a channel, Bonner snapped back to the moment and realized what he was doing. He muttered something inaudible then let me go.

He stood back up and straightened his shop tunic. "Get out," he said without looking at me. I grabbed my book bag and ran from the shop to find Frank.

I found Frank sitting on a bench where other seniors hung out. He was playing the guitar he'd brought with him to school that day. I was so shaken I was stuttering, trying to tell him what had just happened.

Frank looked startled and immediately stopped playing his guitar. He looked up at me standing there shaking.

"What's going on?" he said. He stared at me and listened intently as I told him what had happened. Frank got to his feet, put his hand on my shoulder and said, "Follow me."

I was surprised by how calm he was as he slowly walked us to the shop classroom.

When we walked into the room Bonner was sitting with his hands folded, resting in front of him on his desk. He was staring blankly at nothing, as if in a trance.

Frank motioned for me to hold the guitar and then walked over to one of the tool racks and picked up a pair of pinking shears, the kind used for cutting metal. With shears in hand, he walked over to Bonner who hadn't moved.

Frank leaned in and held the closed pinking shears under Bonner's throat. This time it was Bonner who froze.

"If you ever touch my brother again," Frank said flatly, "I'll cut your throat. Do you understand?" Bonner slowly nodded his head as he looked at Frank with a mixture of fear and loathing.

Frank pulled back his right hand, the one holding the pinking shears. He set the tool down on a nearby workbench. Then, using his wiry body, he climbed up onto the desk and motioned for me to hand him the guitar.

He sat down cross-legged and let the guitar rest in his lap. Frank began to strum while staring at Bonner, who now appeared catatonic. It was the strangest thing I'd ever seen Frank do. My brother, still seated and strumming, looked out the window, seemingly detached.

It was as if he were dissociated from his heroics to protect me. I stood with my jaw hanging open waiting to see what the hell was going to happen next.

Things were frozen in time, like a camera's snapshot. A few minutes passed and then the gym teacher burst into the room followed by the principal, Mr. Lloyd Brusk.

Mr. Brusk calmly said to Frank, "Get off the desk and come with me. Now." Frank looked at them, then at Bonner, then at me. Frank said, "Go on, get to class, Bobby."

But Mr. Brusk said, "No. You're both coming with us." We left the room in single file while dozens of other students lined the halls staring at us in silence as we were led to the Principal's office.

While we walked it felt like a slow motion movie and I was acutely aware of two things. First, my big brother Frank was nobody to fuck with. Second, the kids watching us were in awe.

Being defended by my big brother, and in front of everyone, gave me a rush. I thought about all of the kids who had bullied and taunted us over the years. I thought, "Look at us now, a couple of bad asses."

Even though it was Bonner who had assaulted me, the school felt Frank's actions had overshadowed the teacher's physical and emotional outburst and Frank and I were suspended.

This only validated Frank's worldview that nothing was fair, there's no justice, and you have to fight for what's right.

The principal called Mom and told her that we were being sent home for causing trouble in class and that either she or Dad would have to come in to resolve things.

Next day, Dad was pissed off when he had to take the day off from work to come to the school and deal with the problem.

Frank and I were standing with him at the principal's office door but before we went into the meeting Dad said, "You've gone too far this time. I'm sick and tired of putting up with your bullshit.

Things are going to change around here. I'm not cleaning up your messes anymore." It was his contempt prior to the inquisition that made the whole episode surreal.

The meeting was, at best, a farce. At worst, it was a perfect example of how parents and school officials bulldoze adolescents, harping about adhering to rules and threatening to expel us if we didn't toe the line.

After an hour of posturing, the outright lies by the teacher had the principal hoodwinked. Mr. Tool Box said, "Robert Zappa caused trouble in my class. When I told him to stop it, he lunged at me and I had to restrain him."

Right in front of us, the principal said to Dad, "If Robert had hit his teacher he would've been arrested. Believe me, by restraining him this teacher acted in the child's best interest."

Frank and I were incensed listening to this bullshit, and even angrier that we weren't given an opportunity to tell our side of the story.

Dad sided with the school immediately. In a patronizing tone the principal turned to Frank and me and said, "The school feels your father's punishment will be sufficient to close this matter. Nevertheless, you two are suspended for three days."

Bonner remained in the classroom without reprimand. Thankfully, I was transferred out of woodshop and hoped that was the last time I'd ever have a run-in like that—with him or anybody else.

The consolation was the realization that even though it was the principal and Mr. Tool Box against us, they had nothing to look forward to but old age and retirement.

We would outlast them in both time and energy. Frank and I would move on, leaving all the assholes, especially Mr. Boner and Principal Brusk, in the dust.

CHAPTER ELEVEN

Conflict & Resolution

"The foundation of Christianity is based on the idea that intellectualism is the work of the Devil. Remember the apple on the tree? Okay, it was the Tree of Knowledge. "You eat this apple, you're going to be as smart as God. We can't have that."

~ Frank Zappa

Hey, Hey DeMolay

Throughout our time in Lancaster, Frank and I continued to walk to and from school together. One day while waiting for him in front of the school he came slowly walking toward me from the direction of the gym. As he came closer I saw he had a paper towel in his mouth and it was covered with blood.

"What happened, Frankie?"

"What does it look like?" he said.

"You look like you ran into a fist with your face," I said and laughed but he was not amused.

"Five guys cornered me in the locker room and beat me up. They said it was for going after Mr. Bonner."

The kids who hit Frankie were from the DeMolay—one of the "in" groups at Antelope Valley High.

It's a religious organization sponsored by the Masons for boys between 13 and 21 named after Jacques de Molay, the last Grand Master of the Knights of Templar, the secret society made famous in the movie, "The Da Vinci Code."

The DeMolay in America started in 1919 in Kansas City and expanded its membership throughout the United States under the sponsorship of Masonic Lodges.

Members of the DeMolay are taught seven cardinal virtues: filial love, reverence for sacred things, courtesy, comradeship, fidelity, cleanliness, and patriotism.

I'm not sure where in their scripture it stated that it was their duty to beat the shit out of Frank.

As we walked home, Frank said, "As they were punching me they kept yelling, "We better not catch you again or we're really gonna fuck you up.""

When we got home and walked in the door, Mom saw Frank's bloody lip and her face lost all its color. Mom reached for a towel and ran it under the water.

She went to dab it on Frank's face. He took it out of her hand. He put it on his lip himself. She looked hurt but let him do it anyway.

Panicking, Mom said, "Don't tell your father." I thought, 'Isn't that great.' She was afraid of Dad going ballistic even though it was Frank who had just been assaulted.

We never said anything. Dad got home and as usual went to sit in his chair and smoke. While he was unwinding from the day, he either didn't notice Frank's face or chose to ignore it.

If Frank had said anything, Dad would've yelled at him. He would've blamed Frank for what happened. That meant Frank couldn't tell Dad about the DeMolay guys who beat him up.

He couldn't tell Principal Brusk either because we were already on the school's shit list.

Later that night Frank said to me, "They wouldn't listen to us then, why would they listen to me now?"

Once again, Frank's cynicism of the world was confirmed: he had to deal with the incident all by himself. The message seemed to be, "Shut the fuck up and just suck it up."

The next day when Frank went to gym class, the DeMolay boys didn't bother him. The day after that, same thing—no DeMolay thugs came to beat him up.

Finally, on the third day, one of the kids who'd jumped Frank stopped him outside the gym and said he was sorry for what happened. He told Frank they wouldn't be bothering him anymore.

We found out later that one of my classmates who'd seen Mr. Bonner go crazy on me in woodshop told the DeMolay what happened and how the teacher had freaked out on me.

I'm not sure if it fell under the category of "reverence for sacred things, courtesy, or comradeship" but now the DeMolay respected Frank for defending his little brother. The enemy of my enemy is my friend, unless my friend is still my enemy.

More of the same, only different

As time passed and these two incidents faded from the high school gossip mills, Frank and I fell back into our school routines. We'd walk together in the morning and on most afternoons go back home together.

One afternoon, as we were crossing the athletic field heading home, two boys stood in our way. They had their arms crossed and their jaws jutted out.

One called us "nigger lovers" and the other one took off his jacket to get ready to fight. Frank started to step forward but I put up my arm and blocked his move.

Frank told them, "Fuck off." That's when the guy who'd taken his jacket off took a step toward Frank. I stepped in front of Frank and pulled out the switchblade I got from the guy in Sun Village.

I held the knife out in front of me, pushed the button, and saw the blade fling forward two inches from the kid's face.

Instantly I realized that was a really stupid thing to do. The guy could've easily overpowered me. Thankfully, Frank's instincts were quick and he moved toward me as a back up.

"You touch either one of us and you're gonna lose an eye," said Frank.

I stayed mute and just kept holding the knife up to the kid's face, trying not to shake. The other kid started to back off.

Then he told his friend, "Leave these crazy motherfuckers alone. We'll just tell my Dad they pulled out a knife on us."

That's when Frank turned to that kid and in the same stony calm voice he'd used with Mr. Bonner said, "If you do, my brother and I will find you and slit your throat." The kids scowled and stood there trying to look menacing, but then they turned and hurriedly walked away.

A few nights later Frank and I were sitting in his room listening to 45 rpm records when the doorbell rang. Mom answered and we heard someone ask for Frank. Mom called us and went to see who was at the door.

We didn't recognize the guy standing in the doorway but we could see two other guys were waiting out front. When Frank got to the door, Mom went back to the living room.

Frank said, "Who are you and what do you want?"

"I'm here to kick your ass," the kid said.

Frank didn't flinch, nor hesitate. He walked past the kid in the doorway and stepped outside. He then walked to the driveway in front of our house.

One of the boys hauled off and hit Frank in the face; then he tackled him to the ground. As they wrestled in the driveway, the two other boys started yelling, "Get him! Get that motherfucker!"

I watched, feeling helpless, as the two of them were rolling around on the gravel. Frank's attacker was on top of him punching him in the face.

There was no way for Frank to defend himself from that position. With a sudden burst of courage, or insanity, I ran over and kicked his attacker in the ribs knocking him off of Frank.

The other two boys rushed at me but by then Dad had come outside to see what was happening. The three of them saw him at the door and ran off down the street. They jumped into a car that had been idling, with a fourth kid at the wheel.

They sped off and Dad helped Frank up and into the house. He didn't ask if Frank was okay. He said,

"Serves you right. That oughta teach you not to make so much goddamn trouble at school."

There is more to life than alfalfa

By now, Frank hated Lancaster as much, if not more, than I did. Life was getting progressively worse for us in school and his relationship with Dad was deteriorating rapidly.

There were times when they could hardly stand to be in the same room together.

Dad criticized Frank's "good for nothing music" and called him a fool for spending so much time listening to it.

In an effort to distance ourselves from those turmoil-filled confrontations, we began taking trips down to L.A. with guys from the band. Neither Frank nor I had a driver's license or access to a car so we'd go with Terry Wimberly or the Carters and Johnny Franklin.

We went to the folk music clubs on Melrose Boulevard; the most famous was the Ash Grove.

Ed Pearl ran the Ash Grove and it was where blues legends Brownie McGee and Sonny Terry, and folk singers Odetta and Pete Seeger played.

That's where we spent countless hours listening to some of the best folk and blues music. At the Ash Grove Frank got to know some of the musicians and picked up a lot about performing and the music business in general. It was there that he began to visualize his future in the industry.

When Frank was away from Lancaster he stood up straighter, seemed more mature, and spoke with ease. One Saturday night after Brownie and Sonny's set, Frank went up and introduced himself.

Brownie and Sonny were friendly and welcomed Frank and me to come sit at their table. I followed Frank's lead, mesmerized, as usual, by his confidence.

Brownie talked about knowing Blind Boy Fuller and Leadbelly. His stories about growing up in the South and learning how to play guitar were fascinating. Brownie had a pronounced limp from a childhood injury and Sonny was blind.

At the end of their sets, they walked off stage, Brownie still strumming his guitar and limping and Sonny holding Brownie's shoulder and playing his harmonica.

I felt emotional watching the two black men walk away with dignity after living lives filled with so much indignity, and I realized then that skin color was not the problem.

The problem was the overwhelming ignorance and prejudice that put men like Brownie and Sonny in a separate category, one that denied their true value as musicians and human beings.

Frank had reached that same conclusion much earlier. I could see that in the way the three of them talked like they were old friends. They talked the language of music, and performing, and especially the blues.

On the way home that night, Frank turned toward me. "I know for sure what I'm gonna do with my life," he said. "Music. All music. Fuck Dad."

The Curse of the Demon

Before we moved from Lancaster, Frank and I went to dozens of movies. He loved science fiction but I was still in my Disney cartoon stage—I'd grown bigger but maturity hadn't kicked in yet. One night we saw "Curse of the Demon" at the movie theater starring Dana Andrews and Peggy Cummings.

An American psychologist who doesn't believe in the paranormal goes to London where he finds out his friend is dead and people are blaming it on a Satanist's curse.

The once-skeptical psychologist finds out that he has touched the curse and must pass it on to someone else or he'll be dead, too.

It was the scariest movie I had ever seen. Frank loved it and talked about it for days. When I told Frank how scared I was he said, "It's only a movie, for Christ's sake."

After seeing that movie I had nightmares about the demonic curse coming to get me and woke up in a cold sweat night after night—which, by the way, Frank thought was really funny.

He began telling me there's a whole lot of mystery out there in the sky and planets and stars that we know nothing about. He began reading up on space travel and alien life forms. There were no limits to my brother's curiosity.

Many nights the desert sky was surprisingly clear and it was easy to see planets and stars with an average power telescope.

Frank had made a friend in school who brought over his telescope so he and Frank could stare into the heavens on warm summer nights. They charted the movements of stars on graph paper.

Once Frank came bursting into my room shouting, "I just saw a UFO!". I was convinced Frank's development had entered yet another orbit and that he'd gone deeper into The Twilight Zone—a TV show we never missed.

He also became interested in weird things like the occult and magic. He drew monsters and alien creatures in pencil and charcoal and even wrote a few stories about them. By this time neither of us had attended church for ages.

I began to feel unnerved as I wondered where these bizarre interests of Frank's were headed. He told me one day that he was going to try to find a copy of a book called The Necromancer's Manual.

The Necromancer's Manual was supposed to be a "how-to" reference book for black magic and spells from the Middle Ages. It contained records of court cases of people who were brought up on charges for using magic.

It was also supposed to have instructions on how to devise and use magic spells. Frank's research said necromancy was the most extreme form of magical practice and involved summoning demons. Frank said he wanted to see if it was possible to actually conjure up a demon and make it do his bidding.

That was all too spooky for me but as much as Frank tried to frighten me, and others, I think he was genuinely just curious and having fun.

He never did find a copy of the manual, so I don't know how much further he went with all that later in his life but one time he said cryptically, "I made a bargain with the devil." Maybe that's why he had such bad luck in London, Montreux, and with his health.

CHAPTER TWELVE

Claremont, CA (Again)

"If you want to get laid, go to college. If you want an education, go to the library."

~ **Frank Zappa**

After our years of adolescent psychodrama in Lancaster, Frank graduated from high school in 1959. His experiences at Antelope Valley Joint Union High School turned him off to the idea of continuing on with a formal education.

High school, for Frank, had been a waste of time. He knew what he wanted to do and going to college would only serve as a roadblock to pursuing the path he'd chosen. After what must have been a series of decisions with Mom involving our high school traumas,

Dad's frustration with his job at Edwards Air Force base, and our universal and rapidly growing distaste for Lancaster, Dad told us that he got another job.

This news was actually welcomed, which was also a departure from his many previous announcements about our next move.

This time, when Dad broke the news that we were moving, we could do the relocation routine by rote. Packing up and leaving Lancaster was a breeze compared to all the other times.

It was almost a thrill to be escaping the dry, hot, punishing desert and all the strife that Frank and I ran into that year. So we packed up and we finally left Lancaster. The even better news was that we were moving back to Claremont, California.

Dad's new job was working again for Convair, the defense contractor that he had worked for when we first moved to Claremont.

Our country was shifting into Cold War high gear and employment opportunities in the military-industrial complex were bountiful.

I grew up thinking that there was a never-ending supply of jobs in the defense industry and that Dad was just taking advantage of those opportunities.

Until I got older, it never occurred to me that his frequent job changes might have been the result of his performance at work.

Dad was a proud man and may have bristled at being told what to do, which may have been his cross to bear as an employee in an industry that told everybody what to do and when to do it.

But this was also an era that allowed for employees to have a say in where, how long, and for whom they worked. It was prior to the "Employment at Will" law that granted corporations the right to fire people without explanation or justification.

If you didn't like where you worked or didn't like your boss, you could walk out on your own terms if you had another job to go to.

When the laws changed in favor of corporations, job jumping got harder and salaries began lowering for new employees, regardless of experience.

Dad was ahead of the curve when it came to choosing where he wanted to work even if it meant a lateral career move or another relocation for his family.

As time wore on, I wondered if Dad had been trying to outrun intolerable feelings that plagued him and set him in fight or flight mode.

He had shown no regard for the impact the moves were having on everyone around him. When he got an itch for a new job that would be that. We'd move. He wanted a better house, so we'd move. He saw himself as head of the household. Frank and I saw him as a bully.

Mom once told me that when Dad was at Edwards Air Force Base he had been asked to be part of a classified study in Utah.

It had seemed like a good career move to Mom but he refused the invitation to go for an overnight visit just to see the research site.

The assignment was given to someone else and Dad never gave Mom any explanation for his refusal to explore it.

Turning down this career opportunity probably made him appear unprofessional to his higher ups.

He was taciturn at home and apparently not much different at work. He couldn't understand why his employer wouldn't let him do his part of the research project at Edwards. At the same time he resented being asked to leave his prized television set and comfortable chair.

Dad's petulance probably resulted in us packing up again. Dad's stubborn streak and tendency to roam were handed down to Frank who had to have things his way and who spent months on the road and away from his family.

We were taking with us a collection of memories, good and bad, that had shaped Frank's view of the world, as well as his views of music. During the Lancaster stint Frank went through many personal changes.

He became more cynical about our family's transience. He grew more distrustful of authority. He became more entrenched in his love of music and performing. His creative energies were growing exponentially.

While Frank grew intellectually and musically, I grew more girth. The thinner Frank got, the more my circumference expanded. Other differences between us seemed to be widening also. Frank was quick to recognize and avoid potential pitfalls that could stifle his creativity.

His obsessive, mathematical mind along with his endless hunger for knowledge and a relentless perfectionism were transforming him into what seemed superhuman to me. It was as if I were watching a plane revving up on the runway and about to lift off the ground.

His musical genius was taking off and as we left Lancaster it was clear to me that Frank was moving upward to greater things.

There was a selfish part of me that wanted to hold him back so he'd be there to keep guiding and protecting me.

But I knew that because he had so many interests and was becoming a unique individual he would move on, with or without me.

Maybe you can go home again, sometimes...

As soon as Dad sold our house in Lancaster we headed south. Mom was sad to leave our first—and only—new house. Because of what might have been a combination of resignation and real interest, Mom had grown to like the neighborhood in Lancaster.

I remember the fear in her eyes when this latest move was announced. She was simply exhausted from so many upheavals. But the silver lining for Frank and me was our return to Claremont.

My reactions to this move were only positive. In spite of all that Frank and I went through in Lancaster, I had grown, not just physically, but emotionally and intellectually as well. I became more independent, even though I still looked to Frank for direction.

I was a little more outgoing and had gained enough confidence to offset my awkward adolescent characteristics.

Being fat was one thing, but fat, pimply, and uncoordinated were not good qualities. I was happy about making a fresh start and optimistic about the future.

In a moment of unexpected awareness, Dad must've picked up on Mom's vulnerability because he made the big effort to lessen her stress by finding a house two doors down from our first house on Oak Park Drive.

But, in place of what we expected to be her joy to be back on our old block in Claremont, there was only a stoic acceptance. Even leaving the hellhole named Lancaster wasn't enough to overcome that feeling of long-suffering submission.

Mom had become passive to our transient existence. She had no close friends or support system to rely on.

She had Candy and Carl to tend to and the never-ending weight of trying to please Dad. Mom had little energy left to worry about Frank and me.

The stress of our frequent moves had worn her down. Dad's dying dreams of securing the good life left him sucked dry, withdrawn, and angry.

He continued to smoke heavily and his health began to deteriorate. His breathing was labored and he tired easily.

He had put on a lot of weight and it took him longer to get up out of his chair. He sighed a lot as if to put an exclamation point on how crappy he was feeling.

This was the beginning of a scary time for us. As a younger child I'd been in denial about the impact the moves were having on all of us.

Frank would make observations about how our lives were getting more and more screwed up because of Dad. He often said how much he wished we could stay put for longer than a year or two.

Oddly, after this move Dad began to think more about Frank's future. He wanted Frank to become an engineer. Frank had never shown even an iota of interest in engineering (other than his misadventures with explosives in Monterey).

But Dad became fixated on Frank following in his footsteps.

My brother knew that if being an engineer meant working on military bases, relocating, changing jobs constantly, and living a transient existence, he wanted no part of it. But, as with all of the arguments in the past, the more Frank resisted, the more Dad insisted.

I was surprised when Frank caved. In an effort to make peace Frank enrolled at Chaffey Junior College in Ontario, California. He signed up for courses in English, music, and art.

It wasn't torture for Frank because those were subjects that interested him and he was still a sponge for knowledge and a seeker of new experiences. That decision pacified Dad, but only a little. He continued to badger Frank with put-downs.

Dad's plan was to continue to push Frank towards engineering and to get him to move out of the house. He told Frank that he needed to branch out on his own.

Like many young men during that era, Frank had little practical life experience that would enable him to live alone. The lack of life experience notwithstanding, Frank gave it a shot.

First he had to get a job. Luckily he found a quasi-creative position working for Nile Running Studio, a greeting card company in Claremont.

Frank mostly designed silk-screened greeting cards, designed for elderly women who liked flowers. It was not a very demanding job, he once said.

During his time at Running's Studio, Frank also painted dozens of pictures using acrylics on canvas and plywood. He gave some of those paintings to our mother and she loved them.

One painting that he gave Mom was of an urn; he tried to sell others, but with little success. The designs he did for the card studio were not much of a stretch for him, but his boss and the customers loved them.

Acrylic on Plywood – Painted by Frank

While he was attending Chaffey, Frank met and eventually married his first wife, Kay Sherman, an attractive blonde, almost as tall as Frank. Kay had a great smile and a sophisticated sense of humor. She and Frank hit it off almost immediately.

Early in their relationship Kay gladly supported Frank when he was beginning his music career. But as their finances became an issue, she wanted him to get a steady day job and put music on the back burner.

Before they got married they both dropped out of Chaffey and moved into an old house in Ontario, California.

Kay went to work for a bank and Frank kept working for Nile Running Studios until it was apparent that he and Kay needed more money to maintain their lifestyle.

He took a job writing ad copy and designing newspaper ads for some of the local businesses. He even did one for the bank where Kay worked. But the money from those jobs still wasn't enough, so he took a job selling Collier's Encyclopedias door-to-door.

Like many young couples during that time, settling in and building their nest egg wasn't easy, especially for those without a profession, specific skills, or training.

The fact that they didn't have enough money to do all that they wanted to do, like travel, or go out on the weekends, or even think about a family, began to put a strain on their relationship.

But before the slow deterioration began, Kay was his biggest fan and supporter.

Early in their relationship Kay encouraged Frank to go in directions that he probably would not have gone on his own without her support. She knew he was interested in writing music and she wanted him to pursue his dream.

In the spring of 1961 Frank and Kay went to Pomona College to meet with music professor Karl Kohn. It's never easy to determine the tipping points in one's life, but this may have been an important one for Frank.

That said, I do believe that while Frank truly wanted to pursue a career in music, he might not ever have done so without this turn of events.

Composition at Pomona

Pomona College is one of the top private schools in the country. It's a highly respected liberal arts college in the same league as schools like Amherst, Vassar, Brown, and Swarthmore.

Frank Zappa could never have attended Pomona if admission had been based on his high school record or ability to pay.

Dr. Karl Kohn is a distinguished music professor at Pomona College. He's a Harvard graduate, a Fulbright Scholar, and has earned fellowships from the Guggenheim, Howard, and Mellon Foundations.

Professor Kohn has also received four grants from the National Endowment of the Arts. But, in addition to being that kind of impressive, he also taught composition and music at Pomona and with his wife, Margaret, they performed duo piano concerts all over the U.S. and Europe.

On Kay's suggestion, she and Frank went to Dr. Kohn's office to ask if he would allow Frank to audit his composition course. They explained that they had no money to pay for the course for credit.

They also knew that Frank did not have the grades or the S.A.T. scores that would qualify him for admission to Pomona as a regular student.

But Frank and Kay both knew that Frank needed formal training if he was ever going to become a composer.

In a lengthy phone conversation I had with Professor Kohn, he recalled that when Frank and Kay came to his office, Kay did most of the talking.

He remembered that Frank sat quietly looking around his office being very "respectful."

His most vivid impression of Frank was that he was "very polite, agreeable, even reticent" during the interview.

As it turned out Professor Kohn had already heard about Frank from his colleague, Sylvia Brighton, a musician and music professor at SUNY Buffalo.

She told Dr. Kohn that she knew a "bright young man who exhibited an unusual talent for composition." When Dr. Kohn met Frank he had a feeling that her assessment was accurate.

Frank and Kay's visit, along with the recommendation from Dr. Brighton, resulted in Dr. Kohn allowing Frank to audit his summer class.

According to Dr. Kohn, that summer Frank sat in on his composition class, he never missed a day. When Frank handed in his compositions they were always written in India ink.

That suprised Dr. Kohn because all of his other students used pencil. In his estimation that exhibited how confident Frank was in his abilities.

He realized that Frank was not only competent as a composer, but that he was confident enough in his work to present it in finished form.

He was not intimidated by the fact that he was handing in work to a world famous educator and professional musician. Frank did what was now feeling natural to him.

He did his work with no pretense or ego. He handled the assignments like a professional. His youth and lack of experience seemed a non-issue. Frank learned quickly and retained whatever he'd learned.

Several years later, after Frank was established as a rock musician and the leader of the Mothers of Invention, Dr. Kohn told me that one day he received two tickets in the mail from Frank.

Frank was inviting Dr. Kohn and his wife Margaret to Frank's concert at the Pauley Pavilion at U.C.L.A. Frank had sent the tickets personally and invited Dr. and Mrs. Kohn to stop by backstage after the show.

Dr. Kohn told me that he and his wife were excited about going to the concert and eager to see Frank again. Dr. Kohn said the show was filled with "rough language along with some unusually intricate musical interludes", a pattern that would later become standard for The Mothers of Invention's shows.

He said that he was a bit intimidated and even a little put off by the "vulgarities," but that did not discourage him and his wife from wanting to go backstage and thank Frank personally for the tickets.

When they got in to see Frank, Dr. Kohn recalls being completely taken off guard by Frank's warm welcome. He said Frank was extremely polite, very professional, and courteous.

Frank thanked them for coming and they talked for a while about the show, Frank's direction in music, and life in general. Dr. Kohn thanked Frank for sending him the tickets, wished him well, and left.

That was the last time he saw Frank in person. Dr. Kohn has been interviewed many times about his association with Frank and the influence he might have had on Frank's music.

While Frank worked at becoming a musician, Kay worked as a teller in a bank in Ontario, California. As Frank's creativity grew, Kay became the anchor in their relationship, managing their day-to-day affairs.

Kay may have secretly resented Frank's career choice, inasmuch as he wasn't earning enough money. He was working less and less at day jobs, which compounded their financial problems and Kay's frustration with him.

Frank was concentrating on his music career. Kay was relegated to making enough money to run the household.

Without Kay's support Frank would not have been able to devote as much time as he did to his music. Unfortunately, it would be Frank's devotion to music versus working at a day job that would result in the demise of their marriage.

Frank's leaving home and moving in with Kay turned out to be one of the best things he could have done for Mom and Dad.

His departure freed up household expenses giving our parents a little extra money, which they would need as things got worse for Dad. He lost his job at Convair forcing us to move to another house in the same neighborhood for a lower rent.

Shortly after that move, Dad had a heart attack and remained in the hospital for a week.

This was yet another difficult time for our family. Mom was getting more and more depressed. She seemed listless and distracted.

She was clearly worried about Dad's health and her fears were compounded by her anxiety about Frank, me, Carl and Candy.

Carl was withdrawing, Candy was treading water, and I was getting angrier at the way things were turning out. I didn't know who to be madder at: the businesses that Dad worked for and caused him to make so many changes, or Dad himself for not being like other fathers who were more stable.

After about a week in the hospital Dad came home and began his recovery. But he didn't take too much time doing that because we needed money to live. So he pulled himself together and found another job, but at a lower salary.

We ended up moving one more time while I was still a member of the household.

We moved into an area on the outskirts of the Claremont Colleges complex where mostly Mexican families, day laborers, and college support staff employees lived.

The homes were small with some front and back lawns cluttered with disabled cars on cinder blocks. There was trash in piles and spilling out of barrels, construction materials, and scraps everywhere.

Our place wasn't as bad as the worst but not as good as the best in the area. Mom was now at her lowest point.

She seemed to be tired all the time and didn't show much interest in what was going on with her children, especially me. I was in high school then and completely on my own when it came to schoolwork or extracurricular activities.

Our family was slowly disintegrating. Frank was out of the house so Dad couldn't blame the way he felt on him. With Frank gone he didn't have his first-born son to direct or, in some way, goad into doing what he thought he should do.

During the summer before my senior year I became friends with a few of the neighborhood boys and I enjoyed sneaking out at night to meet them.

The window in my bedroom opened out onto our backyard, which was how I made my nightly exits after everyone was asleep. My new buddies and I would go into the bodega to buy beer and snacks, then go sit by the train tracks eating Fritos and Corn Nuts and drinking the Brew 102 which gave us the runs.

One advantage to living in that area was the lax enforcement of liquor laws.

I remember the late summer night/early morning symphony of fragrances of the lemon and orange blossoms along with the lingering smell of flour and corn tortillas and refried beans mixed with the occasional odor of skunk during those laugh-a-minute benders with my friends

I was accepted because my hair was black and I could eat five corn tacos.

This was not the exclusive club that would impress anybody's parents but these guys were loads of fun and that was good enough for me.

Time to go

As a senior at Claremont High School I began to wonder about my next move in life. I wasn't much of a student, but unlike Frank, who'd tended to be dark and morose, I was having a pretty good time. Dad had given up trying to convince me to do anything after high school. I had no clue which way to go.

I showed no signs of any talents other than mowing lawns and grating cheese at Di Orio's Pizza. Those were my two jobs where I earned pocket money and could make my contribution to the household expenses.

Dad seemed to have no interest in what I was going to do as long as it got me out of the house and no longer cost him money.

As my senior year came to an end I realized that most of the students I knew were applying to college; some had already been accepted.

I had no motivation, and I didn't even know how to begin the tedious process of applying. I was either going to end up in a junior college like Chaffey, where Frank had gone for a while or get a menial job. Neither option was very appealing.

For years I'd wondered why I hadn't been born with Frank's musical talent—or any talent so I'd know what to do with myself.

A few weeks before graduation Dad called me into the living room and said, "I'm going to take a teaching job in Florida so we'll be moving soon. What are your plans?" 'Good lord not another move,' I thought. 'He must be kidding.'

But then Dad's message computed. This was his way of telling me I was on my own. He wasn't inviting me to Florida.

I was being told the family was leaving me. I became disoriented, then angry. I stormed out of the house.

I went for a walk to blow off steam and was plagued by panicky thoughts of being homeless.

I couldn't live with Frank because he and Kay were only getting started and they certainly didn't need me to get in their way.

When I finally told Frank about my talk with Dad, he said, "That's the best thing that ever happened to you." He told me to get my shit together, find a job, and move on with my life.

Not the most encouraging pep talk but it was the kick in the ass I needed to figure out what to do next.

Moving On...

Fortunately, during my senior year at Claremont High School I had joined a Scout troop. I liked doing things with other guys that involved outdoor stuff and I got along well with the boys in the troop.

The leader was Pomona College senior Norm Hines. Norm was the captain of the football team, captain of the swimming team, co-captain of the wrestling team, and when he wasn't captain of something he was majoring in English.

He was also involved with ceramics and sculpture, a true Renaissance man.

Norm did his pottery and sculpture at Scripps College, part of the Claremont Colleges consortium.

Scripps had a ceramics department and several large kilns where students fired and glazed their pots.

One day Norm asked me to stop by the department and help him mix clay. I had nothing else to do so I figured, why not?

Norm and I became friends during those afternoons of mixing clay. One weekend he took our scout troop to a beach in Baja California just below Tijuana, the notorious city south of San Diego.

We camped out on the beach, swam in the ocean, and had a grand time sitting around the campfire at night eating burgers and hot dogs.

This was a great distraction while I stressed about a life raft to grab onto. The only skills I had were making friends and then losing them.

I was yearning for a shred of security, anything that would keep me on course and provide stability.

The Boy Scout troop was keeping me grounded and it provided a much-needed connection.

CHAPTER THIRTEEN

Tijuana, Mexico

"So long as somebody gets a laugh out of it, what the fuck?"

~ **Frank Zappa**

Tijuana is the place Southern California high school seniors are drawn to. It's a pit stop to the seedier side of life before getting your shit together and going to college or into the service. It was a rite of passage.

You had to be on your toes when in Tijuana. Should things get out of hand the notorious Federales were happy to toss another gringo in the Tijuana jail.

If this were to happen it would be a nightmare for the kid's parents and a big headache for the U.S.

Government. The Tijuana jail was where prisoners were held for months before arraignment or trial and there was nothing the U.S. government could do about it.

One weekend before I graduated from high school, my friends Dick Barber, Robert Peters and I drove down to San Diego and across the border into Tijuana.

We wanted to take in a few shows, drink some local beer, and eat authentic Mexican food. It started off innocently enough.

After crossing the border our first stop was the Zona Norte. This was the red light district rife with rundown motels, faux-exotic nightclubs, and bizarre entertainment. We had heard sleazy stories about a performance involving a donkey.

Curiosity roped us in. Robert Peters was sure it was a hoax. I thought the donkey was really a guy in a costume. And we all had doubts about the rumored señorita in the act.

We found a hot spot called Zorro Azul, paid our two dollars at the door, and paid another dollar for a warm Tecate cervesa.

We elbowed our way to the edge of the elevated stage. "No cameras, por favor," the sign read, and no touching the señoritas on stage.

Beefy bouncers with shiny gel in their hair and bad teeth wandered through the crowd to enforce the rules. There'd be no trouble from us. We had no intention of running afoul of the law in this risky foreign land.

The potential dangers in Tijuana were frightening but they made it all the more thrilling and our fears were dwarfed by the excitement of being there. Soon the lights dimmed and the mariachi music began.

The first act was a woman identified over the crackling loudspeaker as the "Lovely Miss Lindsey." Miss Lindsey looked more like a linebacker than the hot exotic dancer we'd expected to see for the $2.00 admission fee.

With a cigarette dangling from her lips and her boxy body glistening with sweat, she looked like a bouncer at one of the Claremont barrio bars. Miss Lindsey Linebacker began to bump and grind, working the stage like a humping dog in heat.

Dick Barber let out a loud choking laugh. Beer came squirting out of my nose and Robert Peters put a hand in front of his eyes to block her from his view.

A man standing next to Robert reached up and tried to grab Miss Lindsey's underpants—a breach of the house rules. Lucky for him, he missed and Miss Lindsey pranced on.

After she evaded her admirer's grasp, Miss Lindsey moved around the stage to the delight of the other men standing six-deep at her feet.

She continued her gyrations until she was back in front of Robert, Dick, and me. As she approached Robert she reached down and smacked him hard on the side of his face.

The crowd roared and shouted spirited cheers in Spanish as Miss Lindsey sauntered off on her second trip around the stage.

Instead of getting angry and throwing us out the bouncers laughed along with the rest of the hombres in the bar. That was a mistake on their part.

Miss Lindsey's uncoordinated gyrations were whipping the crowd into a crotch-warming frenzy. Her rotation around the stage brought her back within arm's reach of our amigo, Robert.

I suddenly got a very bad feeling and knew that something unpleasant was about to happen.

As she made her way around the bar and back in front of us again, Robert reached up and grabbed the front of her panties.

He got more than he bargained for when along with the panties came a few strands of Miss Lindsey's black pubic hair. She, of course, let out a bullring-volume scream.

In an instant the bouncers were muscling their way toward us. The crowd was scattering while we tried frantically to push our way to the exit.

Meanwhile Miss Lindsey was still screaming and rubbing her crotch, and the bar patrons were laughing hysterically. My beer-filled bladder was about to betray me. Pandemonium was in the air.

Dick was the first one out the door followed closely by me, and then Robert. We ran separate ways while being chased by separate bouncers.

For thirty terrifying minutes we ran around the streets of Tijuana evading the bouncers who were hot on our tails. I was on the lookout for the authorities that could drag us into the Tijuana jail.

Terrified beyond description, I was also now painfully aware that this was a spectacularly stupid thing to have done.

It was like a kick in the balls: I realized that my life would have gone straight down the Tijuana sewer if I had been caught and that was a real wake up call.

I finally spotted Robert and Dick who were hiding in an alleyway on the lookout for me and the Federales. The three of us spotted each other and began waving feverishly. We quickly convened and walked briskly to the car we'd left parked near the U.S. border.

We knew we'd be home free if we could just get to the car. Gingerly we dodged and weaved our way past the taco vendors, nightclubs, and whorehouses to get to the car.

We made it, jumped inside, locked the doors, and high-tailed it toward the U.S. border and the glorious red, white, and blue freedom we had taken for granted. That was our first and last trip to the thrills in Tijuana and we forever erased the lady and the donkey from our to-do list.

I counted that experience as part of growing up without Frank there to tell me how stupid I had been for getting that close to disaster. I realized I could probably make it on my own if I kept my impulses under control.

CHAPTER FOURTEEN

San Diego and the Marine Corps

"Fact of the matter is, there is no hip world, there is no straight world. There's a world, you see, which has people in it who believe in a variety of different things. Everybody believes in something and everybody, by virtue of the fact that they believe in something, use that something to support their own existence."

~ Frank Zappa

Life After High-School

I finally graduated from high school in the summer of 1961. Soon thereafter my parents, Carl, and Candy left for Florida. Norm Hines, my friend from

Pomona College, and his new wife, Anne, invited me to live with them until I sorted out my next move.

Norm had already graduated and Anne was finishing her undergraduate degree at Pomona. I called Frank and let him know where I was.

Even though we were in different towns we kept in close touch. Frank asked me to call back soon to let him know how I was doing.

As things progressed, I got a job at the College Press in Claremont, the company that printed the local newspaper and handled a variety of other specialty jobs.

My assignment was melting lead for the linotype machine and cleaning the shop after hours. When I told Frank about my job he said, "Sounds like you're getting your shit together." That was his form of high praise.

The next thing I did was get accepted to the California State Polytechnic University in Pomona. In those days, admission to a California state school was almost guaranteed. The fact that I had graduated with barely a "C" average proves that point.

Before my folks left, Dad helped me buy car, a vintage Citroen that didn't cost much, only $75. It was the French version of a station wagon. Mine looked like a midget Quonset hut on wheels.

The car was painted a rust color and the driver's seat was an aluminum lawn chair—seriously. The original seat had been removed and might have been in the living room of the guy who owned the car before me.

The gearshift handle protruded from the dashboard making it awkward to use. There was no radio and the windows did not roll up or down but could be opened up half way and latched to allow air in.

There was no air conditioner. This car was even worse than the Henry J, but it was all I could afford and it got me where I wanted to go.

Driving a foreign car with an aluminum lawn chair for the driver's seat apparently was not illegal and I was never ticketed, or even stopped, for this offense.

I drove the Citroen very carefully to and from school. I didn't want it to end up crushed like my bike. Sometimes I drove to see Frank and Kay in Ontario.

Occasionally I drove Frank around when Kay had their car at work. He didn't particularly like riding with me; the passenger's seat was also a lawn chair and Frank had his standards.

When Frank had enough money, he bought a Rolls Royce. He showed me some of the automotive innovations that the Rolls Royce was famous for, like a real automatic transmission and doors with up-and-down windows.

These and other fancy-schmancy improvements in automotive design made the Citroen and the Henry J seem like rolling death traps.

I attended college, but had difficulty focusing on my coursework. I still had not mastered the study habits needed to complete assignments and I was getting frustrated with my lack of progress.

I maintained my job for a while before realizing that I was only marking time. Worse yet, I was imposing on Norm and Anne's privacy so, not knowing what else to do, I decided to look into joining the military.

I went down to the recruiter's offices in Pomona and talked to the representatives from the Air Force and the Army. Neither of them were enthusiastic about having me among their ranks, so I went to talk to the Marine Corps recruiter.

As I walked into the office the Staff Sergeant, who looked like a linebacker, sat behind a desk. I immediately felt like he had been waiting for me all morning. He showed me sexy, glossy brochures, and bragged about all the places he had served.

He got up from behind his desk, put his huge ape-like hand on my shoulder and said, "Young man, you're exactly the kind of recruit the Marine Corps is looking for. When can you start?"

"Um, uh, I'll have to think about it," I stammered. "We can have you on a bus to boot camp in a week!"

The Sergeant sounded so excited I half expected him to burst into a maniacal laugh like the Coachman in the Pleasure Island scene from Disney's "Pinocchio."

I pictured myself, and hundreds of other "lost boys" marching right into a trap, only to be turned into jackasses.

I began to rethink college and how I might make that work as I left the recruitment office. I rewarded myself for not giving in to the Marine Corps mystique by going to a bar in Cucamonga and having a few beers.

After my third, I thought, 'What the hell was I thinking? How could I ever give up this good civilian life for the Marines?'

The next day, however, the Marine Corps recruiter showed up at Norm and Anne's place looking for me.

I told him that I was not sure about enlisting but I was intrigued by his interest. Nobody had ever shown that much interest in me.

Although it was flattering, I had a bad feeling about growing tensions in South East Asia. I was concerned that perhaps this might not be the best time to enlist.

Even I could read the warnings in the newspaper and watch the escalating events on the TV news.

The recruiter must have anticipated my reluctance and said, "There's never going to be a better time to join than right now. The Marines are looking for young men to send to exotic places to serve as embassy guards."

He said I might qualify for that assignment given my educational background (three whole months of college) and he would personally recommend me for Sea School, the elite training program for Marines who worked at U.S. embassies around the world.

It sounded tempting. I could see myself in a U.S. embassy in some exotic place, like Italy or maybe France, wearing dress blues and carrying a side arm looking very serious and totally desirable to the ladies. Southeast Asia seemed less important.

Ever the dreamer, I was about to take the plunge when my friend Dick Barber happened to stop by during the recruiter's sales pitch.

Dick was a co-captain on the football team at Claremont High and is over six feet tall. When the recruiter saw him he quickly shifted his attention from me and began hustling Dick about joining the Corps.

He said we could both go to Sea School, and maybe even end up at the same embassy, if we joined right then. Dick was a lot smarter and better at smelling rats than I was and he politely declined.

I was a sucker for the recruiter's Sea School sweet talk. Without even talking to Frank I decided that I was ready to enlist.

After watching Dick turn down a great opportunity to go to a specialized school and end up in an exotic foreign land guarding a U.S. embassy, I figured I'd show him and everybody else who was smarter.

The second I signed the enlistment papers, the recruiter's attitude changed. He said, "You will go to the processing station in Los Angeles on Wilshire Boulevard at 6:00 a.m. one week from Saturday and be sure you have all of your civilian affairs in order, because you won't be returning to Claremont for quite some time."

He gave me a self-satisfied grin like a used car salesman who'd just sold me a clunker. He shook my hand and said, "Good Luck," walked out the door, and I never saw him again. Suddenly I had the feeling that I had just made an idiotic mistake.

Later that day I called Frank and told him what I had done and his reactions were mixed. He said, "You should've talked to me first." He added that I was now on my own and that, if nothing else, I would learn useful skills.

Marine Corps Recruit Depot – San Diego

As instructed I sorted out my civilian affairs. I quit school, gave notice at my job, sold my Citroen for $50, packed a suitcase with a few civilian clothes, thanked Norm and Anne for putting up with me, and on Saturday morning boarded a bus at 4:30 a.m. headed to the processing station in Los Angeles.

Upon arrival I saw hundreds of other new recruits, all of whom looked like they shared my suspicions they'd made the biggest mistake of a lifetime.

We recruits were all herded into medical and dental exam rooms for physical check-ups and screening for induction.

Next I was fingerprinted and then sworn in to the U.S. military. Next we were ushered into a holding pen to hurry up and wait.

Two long, anxious hours later we were taken to the cafeteria and given a sandwich, potato chips, and a soda. After that measly meal we were separated into buses and transported to San Diego for the Marine Corps Recruit Depot.

Others went to the Navy's boot camp and still others to Army training. It was all very efficient, all very military.

By the time we finished the induction process and got on the bus to San Diego it was 9:00 p.m. It was 11:00 p.m. when we pulled up in front of the new recruit receiving barracks and the shit hit the fan.

The bus door opened and there stood Corporal Steadman, one of our drill instructors.

He stepped up into the bus and started screaming, "Get your sorry asses up and off this bus, maggots! Turn 90 degrees and line up single-file on the sidewalk. Move it!"

That's the moment I was sure I had made a horrible decision. I found myself wishing we'd been arrested in Tijuana. If I'd had a record they never would've accepted me into the Marine Corps. That would've saved me.

While being screamed at by a testosterone-riddled Corporal, Frank and Kay were ending their relationship, Mom and Dad were settled in Florida, and all of my male friends with any brains were working on their military deferments.

Our next stop was the base barbershop where in less than a minute all the hair on my head was lying on the floor. We were marched to the supply room and given a sea bag: two pairs of boots, two sets of utility fatigues, underwear, two hats, and a laundry bag.

It was now 1:00 a.m. Sunday morning. I was looking forward to a good night's sleep and sorting out this horrible mistake with whoever was in charge.

Sleep was not forthcoming just yet. At 1:30 a.m. we were marched to the recruit barracks and given a few minutes to stow our gear in the big wooden footlockers at the end of the bunk beds. Then we were told to get some sleep. There were no bed linens, just soiled mattresses and dirty pillows.

We each jumped onto a rack that we assumed would be ours for the duration. I fell asleep within minutes. Sleep lasted only three hours.

At 4:30 a.m. Corporal Steadman came into the barracks, turned on the lights, and screamed, "Alright you pussies, out of the sack. I will see you on the company street in ten minutes. You will be in full utility dress for the day."

Corporal Steadman was the poster boy for the fabled Marine Corps drill instructor. He was over six feet tall, impeccably starched, bald, clean-shaven, wiry, and mean as a scorpion.

He was one of three other DIs who were assigned to our recruit platoon and he was by far the toughest.

We were all disoriented having just woken up. Most had no idea where they were. I quickly pulled on my boots, pants and shirt, and jammed my hat on as I ran out the door. Unfortunately, I ran right into Corporal Steadman.

I quickly apologized but to no avail. He stood there screaming at me. He said: "Uncover, maggot!" meaning he wanted me to take my hat off, then he took out his empty canteen and hit me over the head with it.

It made a loud clanking sound, which produced a large knot along with a headache. I made a mental note to report him to whoever was in charge.

I fully intended to explain to someone that this was all a big mistake and that I would be going home now, thank you very much.

Of course that never happened. Once your name is signed on enlistment papers, you're theirs. For the next eight weeks I went through Marine Corps boot camp. I asked myself how Frank would have handled this. What would he do?

But all I could think of was the never-ending fights between him and Dad and how there were no winners in those contests of wills.

Interestingly, when I looked around at the sea of disoriented and badly shaken recruits, I suddenly realized that having been uprooted so many times in my life, over and over again, I could handle all of this confusion. I had become immune to upheaval.

I felt sorry for the other guys who came from stable families and had probably never left their hometown. They were really struggling.

For me, packing up and going into the Marine Corps was simply another move. Not a great move, perhaps, but just another move.

So I did as I was told. I soon learned how to keep a low profile, follow instructions, watch how others handled their training, and I actually began liking the discipline and routines we were learning.

I was becoming part of something great, something bigger than myself. I was becoming a Marine.

Now that I knew it was futile to protest, my thoughts focused less on getting out of the Corps and I turned my attention to going to Sea School and working in one of those embassies the recruiter told me about.

Basic training ended and we were sent to the rifle range and advanced infantry training at Camp Pendleton. Marine Corps Base Camp Pendleton is located between the towns of Oceanside and San Clemente north of San Diego.

Camp Pendleton was established in 1942 to train Marines for service in World War II. The base is named after Marine General Joseph Henry Pendleton.

Today it is the home of the 1st Marine Expeditionary Force and other training commands. If there is such a place known as Hell (other than Lancaster) then this was it.

Since personal phone calls were not permitted during the first eight weeks of boot camp, I was only able to write to Frank about boot camp so he knew when my training would end and when and where I would be graduating.

When he got my letter he contacted a few of my friends from high school and together they came down to San Diego for the graduation ceremony. It was the first time I had seen him in almost three months.

Frankie and Bobby after Bob's graduation from Marine Corps boot camp in San Diego.

I was a lot thinner, better nourished, stronger, meaner (a requirement of the job), and a lot more confident.

I was so happy to see Frank and proud of my accomplishments. I was now a full-fledged Marine, or as we later realized, cannon fodder.

I wanted to show my older brother that I was doing okay now and officially on my own, so to speak. I was U.S. Government property for the duration of my enlistment, but nevertheless, I had grown up.

When I saw Frank we hugged and looked at each other for the first time as adults. We had come a very long way from Baltimore and we were no longer the little kids who played and fought and stood by each other during tough times.

Seeing my high school pals was great, too, but seeing Frank was special.

I realized that my misgivings about never being part of a community or being out of step with everyone else, were evaporating. I was part of a legendary military organization and I did, in fact, have a brother who cared about me and whom I cared about. My world was taking shape nicely.

After the pomp and circumstance of the graduation ceremony, Frank said, "I'm really proud of you and I hope you kill all your enemies before they get to you."

I knew he wasn't in favor of the growing conflict in Vietnam but his comment was his way of saying that it was going to get a lot worse and that I had better watch my ass.

I think he might have even been afraid for me but there was nothing either of us could do but let it play out.

Frank said, "Kay and I are finished. She wanted me to get a real job." I understood right away. I knew he was too far into his passion for composing and performing to end up working in a bank.

"Mom and Dad are thinking about moving back to California," Frank said. He rolled his eyes and said, "The more things change, the more they stay the same, eh?"

I shook my head and said, "I can't believe they're even considering another move. That's nuts. Poor Candy and Carl."

The graduation festivities included a light buffet of sandwiches and beverages from the mess hall so we all got some food and found a picnic table to sit around and talk. My friends were curious about my boot camp experience and if I knew where I was going next.

I told them I thought that Sea School was on the docket, but I didn't know for sure. They said they hoped I got it and then we talked about what had been happening in Claremont over the last three months.

Not much, as it turned out, so after a while we were all talked out and they began getting ready to leave. I was sad about Frank and Kay and I told him so, but he did not give me the impression he was that upset about it.

There were handshakes and hugs all around, but when Frank and I hugged I held him a little longer.

I wasn't sure where I would be going for my first duty station and I didn't know when I'd see Frank again.

All of my earlier feelings about community and brotherhood and being part of something big were again on shaky ground.

After Frank and my friends left to go back home I went back to the barracks to pack my sea bag and check the duty roster to see what my next assignment would be. I was certain that it was going to be Sea School. Sadly, it wasn't.

I was assigned to the division of amphibious warfare at Camp Pendleton. In other words, I was going to be a grunt in a rifle platoon that would be training to make a landing either by sea or by helicopter in an area of conflict. That meant Vietnam.

It wouldn't be long before that training would be put to work. I was furious about being lied to. Frank and I had been lied to all our lives. I couldn't believe that now my government had no qualms about lying to me. I felt betrayed, angry, and disillusioned.

I had to face the facts: I'd been naïve and foolish. My first assignment was with the 1st Marine Expeditionary Brigade.

This brigade was created by President Kennedy to set up the blockade around Cuba during the missile crisis in 1962.

After three months of sailing around Cuba, and two landings for training on the island of Vieques, (the side the Navy wasn't using for target practice), we were sent home. Khrushchev blinked, Kennedy smiled, and the rest of the world took a breather. The crisis had ended. Not long after the missile blockade deployment my unit shipped out to Okinawa for more training before we were sent to Vietnam. Sea School my ass.

Boot camp in San Diego is where they make "Hollywood Marines".

CHAPTER FIFTEEN

Cucamonga, CA

"Music is the only religion that delivers the goods."

~ **Frank Zappa**

Before shipping out to Okinawa, and while I was still stationed at Camp Pendleton, Mom, Dad, Candy, and Carl moved back to California from Florida. Mom was unhappy in Florida.

She hated the heat and humidity and missed the California lifestyle, but the real reason may have been that Dad was unable to maintain a job there. They packed up and headed west again.

Once they arrived in California, Dad came up with another business plan. He called his brother, Joe, in Baltimore and suggested that they go into the restaurant business. Dad always wanted to open a pizza parlor.

He loved eating as much as I did. His brother thought it was a good idea for siblings of an Italian famiglia. Uncle Joe packed up his family and moved to California, now being overrun with Maryland Zappa's.

Dad and Uncle Joe were able to get enough financing together and bought a restaurant called The Pit. It was an established burger and fries joint in Upland, California.

Dad thought it wise to stick with that menu for the time being. He and Joe planned to introduce pizza and pasta dishes once they got the hang of running the business.

Mom worked in the kitchen and at the counter while Dad and Joe cooked and served. It was hard work at a time when they should've been looking forward to retiring and taking it easy, but they had few options.

Dad was too old for the jobs in the defense industry, so they invested their meager savings into the restaurant.

Frank became interested in the restaurant because he saw it as a venue for playing music. By then he was with a band that played rock and roll from the

'50s and '60s and he proposed to Dad and Uncle Joe that they have music on the weekends.

Upland is not far from Claremont and on Friday and Saturday nights there were hundreds of students from the seven Claremont Colleges looking for someplace to get together and party. The Pit became known as the place to be.

Frank came up with the idea of putting bamboo shades on the windows to create ambiance—a dark and sinister ambiance, but ambiance nonetheless.

He set up a stage that had a bamboo backdrop but the Upland fire department gave Dad notice that the bamboo was a fire hazard. He was told to remove it or be closed down.

So much for the Italo-Polynesian motif. After that, the décor remained the traditional, non-descript Upland diner motif and the verve was lost, as was the music. Frank and the other musicians found other bars to play in.

Dad and Uncle Joe began making pizza from scratch. They used their Sicilian culinary experiences to create the pies.

OK, so maybe not strictly Sicilian; one of their signature dishes was peanut butter pizza. But the business was slowly beginning to eke out a profit.

The peanut butter pizza wasn't a big seller but it attracted curious customers who would inevitably end up buying burgers instead.

I was floating around Cuba during this period so, sadly, I never got to try the signature PB pizza. I have always liked peanut butter but having it on pizza now sounds, well, awful.

While all that was taking place, Frank reconnected with our high school English teacher, Mr. Donald Cerveris, who had written a screenplay called Run Home Slow and he asked Frank to write the music for it.

The movie, a western, was produced and directed by Tim Sullivan and starred Mercedes McCambridge.

Reviews of the film included words like "stinkeroo" and "must-not-see" but they all said Frank's music was the best part of the film.

Frank used the money he made from Run Home Slow to buy an electric guitar and make a down payment on Pal Studio in Cucamonga.

He renamed it Studio Z. Frank was now on his way into the music and film business. I was still stuck in the Marines.

By October of 1964 I had completed a 15-month tour of duty in the Far East that began with training in Okinawa and ended with a stint in Vietnam.

My unit was sent in after the U.S.S. Maddox and the U.S.S. Turner Joy were fired upon in the Gulf of Tonkin in the South China Sea.

At the time, the Marine Corps had a policy that stated that enlisted men in a time of undeclared war, with less than 120 days of active duty remaining, could be released from active service.

I had 118 days left on my enlistment so I was eligible for release.

As our replacements were being shipped into the harbor at Da Nang, I was boarding a Military Sea

Transport with 3,000 other Marines headed for San Diego. I was one of the lucky ones.

The trip home took eight days. It could have taken six months and I wouldn't have cared. Most of us knew that Vietnam was going to get a lot worse and we were glad to be going home.

After a brief stateside leave, they rounded up the Marines who had 120 days or more left in their hitch and sent them back to Vietnam for another tour.

Some of those men ended up spending another 12 to 15 months in Vietnam. Many of the Marines in my old unit never made it home after their second tour. And many of those who did suffered physical and mental trauma that's taken years to heal. Some never healed at all.

When our ship docked in San Diego, I watched as the relatives, parents, friends, and loved ones of returning Marines waited for them on the pier. Some had come from as far away as New York and Chicago.

My parents, who were living only a hundred miles away in Montclair, California, were not among them, probably because Dad didn't like crowds or maybe he was too overcome with emotion about my returning—I like to think he, at least, cared.

But my brother Frank was there. He had been there when I graduated from boot camp and he was there when I came home. His support meant a lot to me.

CHAPTER SIXTEEN

Pomona, CA

"The United States is a nation of laws: badly written and randomly enforced."

~   **Frank Zappa**

After mustering out of the Marine Corps I moved to Pomona with Gery Gomez, a buddy I served with in the Far East. Gery's father was Vernon Louis Gomez, known to millions of New York Yankee fans as Lefty.

Gery and I rented an apartment in Pomona, and I started looking for work. We also talked about going to college.

I had taken a course in western civilization from the extension program at U.C. Berkeley during my early years in the Marines, and I decided I wanted to major in history.

I went back to California State Polytechnic University in Pomona, applied for reinstatement, and was accepted for the following year.

Gery, who wanted to major in business, applied there, too, and was also accepted. We both found jobs.

I got a job as a clerk at a steel mill in Fontana, California and Gery got a job in a sporting goods store. Then we began the task of getting our bachelor-pad lives on the fast track.

One Saturday Gery said that his dad was coming by to visit, and he wanted me to meet him. I was really looking forward to meeting this living legend.

Although I didn't follow baseball, I knew who Lefty Gomez was. Everybody knew who he was. When he arrived Gery introduced us and I was pleasantly surprised to find that he was the most gracious and outgoing celebrity I had ever met. Of course, I had not met any celebrities before Lefty!

Lefty brought with him a young man who was not only a baseball player but also an actor. That young man, Kurt Russell, would be the second real celebrity I would meet, and he was as friendly as his mentor, Lefty.

Kurt's baseball career began a few years later in the early 1970s when he played second base for the minor league franchise of the California Angels.

It was a short-lived sports career. Kurt was hit in the shoulder by another player while running to second base, a collision that tore the rotator cuff in his shoulder.

This injury forced him to retire from baseball in 1973. It could have been worse. Kurt returned to acting full-time and the rest is movie history.

Our day-to-day routines fell into place with me going to work during the week, and on the weekends driving down to San Diego to see Marcia Lesheski, a psych nurse at a hospital in San Diego. I had met Marcia through another high school pal, Fred Morris.

The night we met Marcia was coming home from work after the 7:00 to 11:00 pm shift, and she told Fred and me that one of her patients had run away from the hospital and she was worried that he might come looking for her.

Having just come back from Vietnam, and after a pretty full night of drinking beer with my friend, Fred, I did what I was trained to do.

I climbed up on the roof of Marcia's bungalow, checked out the fields of fire, then climbed down and set up several booby traps involving empty beer cans, rocks, and string.

Then I secured the windows in her house, sharpened a few knives and placed them near the front door, then sat down and promptly fell asleep.

Fred told me later that Marcia thought I was adorable—weird, but adorable. I figured that any woman who could put up with my nonsense was either desperate or maybe actually liked me. So, after a few months of dating, Marcia and I decided that we would move in together.

In October of 1964, she left her job in San Diego and moved up to Pomona, where we found an apartment in the complex where Gery and I lived. In

January of 1965 we were married in a small ceremony at the Unitarian Church in Montclair, California.

My Mom, Dad, Carl, Candy, Frank and Kay, and a small group of our friends attended the ceremony.

Frank and Kay had already split and were in divorce proceedings but Frank wanted her to be with him for the wedding. After the ceremony we had a small reception at our apartment.

Frank and Kay came, as did Mom, Candy and Carl, and some of our friends from the ceremony. Nothing fancy or elaborate because we didn't have the money to do anything more.

Frank said that he hoped my marriage worked out better than his did. Frank and Marcia got along from the start and later, after a strange turn of events, she was more than happy to have him stay with us for a while.

Not long after our wedding, and by then separated and undergoing the trauma of divorce, Frank moved into what would become known as "Studio Z" on Archibald Avenue in Cucamonga, California, where I would visit him often.

In the evening we sat around and talked about the music he was writing for his screenplay.

It was called "Captain Beefheart vs. the Grunt People." It was going to be a science fiction movie but it never got out of the early stage of development.

One day there was an article in the Ontario Daily Report about Frank and his unusual studio, which he believes caused the San Bernardino Sheriff's department to take notice of him and Studio Z.

That was most likely when Detective Willis and the San Bernardino Sheriff's department hatched their plan to ask Frank to make a porno movie. More on that in a minute...

Anyway, when Frank and I got together we'd have a few beers and listen to rhythm and blues records from the '50s. Occasionally Don Vliet would stop by.

It was always an amusing and unpredictable evening with Don. We would go late into the night, just talking and listening to records like our days in Lancaster.

Frank would go into detail about the Captain Beefheart movie, his plans for making other movies, and sometimes he'd talk about the church across the street. He said that it was a "holy roller" church and, from what he could tell, the people who went there were suspicious of him and his studio.

He thought their reactions to his studio probably stemmed from the blacked out windows and his hand painted sign that gave the vague impression that maybe something dark and sinister was going on inside.

Our evenings at Studio Z were pure entertainment for me because Frank's enthusiasm and creativity were such a great inspiration. I could see the world through his gloriously vivid imagination.

He could make me feel that anything was possible to create through pure ingenuity and attention to detail.

After Kay, Frank, now 24, became involved with a woman named Christine, 19, who would often allude that she was a witch.

Her nickname was Pete. It wasn't long before Frank and Pete ran into a little trouble.

One day a guy came to Frank's studio and asked my brother to make him a porno movie. He even told Frank which sex acts he wanted performed. He asked for a threesome, one on one, girl and girl, adult toys.

My brother didn't have enough money to eat in those days, so, eager to make a quick buck, Frank agreed to do the job for payment of 100 dollars.

That agreement turned out to be a very expensive one for Frank.

Since Frank didn't have a movie camera, he decided to entice Mr. Horny with an audiotape. What Frank didn't know was that his "customer" was actually an undercover detective from the San Bernardino County sheriff's office.

Anxious to make the bust, the detective, whose last name was Willis, agreed to pay for an audiotape. That should have been a warning sign for Frank. How desperate was this guy for sexual stimulation that he would settle for noises instead of images?

When Frank told me about the deal we pictured Willis and a group of his buddies sitting around, drinking beer, and listening to grunts and moans while their imaginations ran amok. But were we wrong!

As Frank was making the deal with Willis, the detective was wearing a wire, and their conversation was recorded by and broadcast to cops in a surveillance truck parked outside the studio. It was all very Dick Tracy.

When Willis came by Studio Z the next day to pick up the tape, he only had fifty dollars with him. Frank told Willis that he wouldn't give him the tape for less than the hundred they had agreed upon, and he pulled the tape away from Willis' hands.

Wanting desperately to make the bust, Willis gave a signal to his backup to swarm in on my brother, the perp.

No SWAT teams, water cannons, tear gas, or armored vehicles were used. Willis's backup consisted of a newspaper photographer and several sheriff deputies who pushed their way into the studio.

They handcuffed the skinny, perpetually hungry Frank, and the wicked witch Pete.

It was a slow fucking news day in Cucamonga so the photographer snapped a photo that appeared on the front page of the local paper.

The men from the sheriff's office confiscated all the tapes in Frank's studio and an 8mm projector that they said was evidence of his nefarious, lust-driven illegal activities.

After slapping each other with high fives, the brave men of law enforcement formally arrested Frank and Pete-Lorraine and took them before a judge to be arraigned.

His self-imposed moral high ground allowed Det. Willis to ignore the 14th Amendment of the U.S. Constitution.

Briefly stated, the Amendment says:

"Section. 1. ...No State shall make or enforce any law, which shall abridge the privileges or immunities of citizens of the United States; nor...deprive any person of life, liberty, or property, without due process of law...."

Due process and equal protection my ass.

Frank and Pete were put in jail for making an audiotape with grunts and moans on it. It just doesn't get any more ridiculous than that.

This was not long after Dad's heart attack and since Frank had no money, Dad took out a loan for Frank's bail.

Frank tried to get the ACLU to defend him because he believed that this was a clear case of entrapment, but the ACLU said his case wasn't significant enough, so Dad had to hire a lawyer.

Dad was hemorrhaging money and was furious at Frank about the mess.

Even though Dad was going through a pretty difficult time then, he still came through for Frank, but not without letting him know how stupid he thought he had been.

Meanwhile, the sheriff's department locked Studio Z up and the City of Cucamonga was now able to breathe easier with the arch criminal and dangerous audiotape maker, Frank Zappa, out of the picture.

After 10 days they got out of jail, and because they had nowhere else to go, Frank and Pete came to stay with Marcia and me at our apartment in Pomona.

We had a second bedroom we let them use, and the afternoon they arrived they were physically and psychologically exhausted from their run-in with the law.

Frank and Pete just wanted a hot shower and some sleep. Later, when they got up, we had dinner and Frank told us about his time in jail. He said he'd been charged with conspiracy to commit pornography.

The pornography part was a misdemeanor but the conspiracy part was a felony, so he was, as he put it, in really deep shit.

He said that his 10 days in jail were the worst experience of his life. He was in with actual criminals who probably belonged there and with others, like him, who had been unjustly accused, arrested, and locked up.

One of the actual criminals Frank met was a guy who was in for stealing copper from the rail yards in the area. One of the other arrestees was a young Mexican boy who had committed the serious offense of jaywalking. Some crime days were slower than others in Cucamonga back then.

Although jail was a nasty experience for Frank, he was more furious about how it all took place. He was angry about the situation, and about how he was sent up the river for what amounted to a stupid mistake.

The entire episode contributed to Frank's growing cynicism about and distrust in the establishment. It was probably also the genesis for many of the songs he would later write.

The San Bernardino Sheriff and district attorney's office wanted to charge Frank with the felony part of his indictment but when the judge heard the tape in chambers he laughed and told the prosecutor to reduce the charge to a misdemeanor.

He said that prosecuting Frank would be a waste of the court's time and money, so the prosecutor reluctantly reduced the charge and Frank ended up with probation.

The lesson it taught Frank was that the legal system in San Bernardino, and probably elsewhere in the country, could be as corrupt as it wanted to be and there was nothing he could do about it.

Frank and Pete stayed with us for several days before they decided to go their separate ways. Their relationship was put on hold and for Frank there wasn't much left to salvage after their ordeal.

When Frank tried to get some of his personal belongings from the studio, the City of Cucamonga refused to allow him back into the building. The Cucamonga city government, as it turned out, had planned to demolish the building and widen the street.

The motive behind the operation seemed clear. Frank was locked out of the building and his equipment and personal belongings destroyed.

The city didn't care about Frank Zappa or Studio Z. They just wanted him out of the building so they could widen the road in their quest to make Cucamonga more attractive as a family-oriented community.

After that, in a fit of disgust, Frank decided to move away from Cucamonga, Pomona, and the entire

San Bernardino area to Echo Park, which was closer to L.A.

It was now 1965. Frank was at a low point in his life. He was on his own, single again, and without enough support or the resources to reestablish himself.

He found a job selling records at a place called Wallach's Music City in Los Angeles, and he began the slow, tedious road back to at least some degree of normalcy.

I visited him a few times at his apartment in Echo Park and was disturbed by the squalor and disorganization.

I was worried about him. He was rail-thin and smoked more than he ate. He drank cup after cup of coffee, and when we got together and I took him out for a burger, he ate like he hadn't had a meal in days, which was probably the case.

As it would turn out I would not have to worry long. Frank was determined to get his life back on track. And when Frank Zappa was determined to make changes, changes were on the way.

Those changes involved the formation of the Mothers of Invention and his emergence as an avant-garde musician and social critic.

From a troubled kid to an almost convicted felon, my brother rose to rock and roll icon status. Frank Zappa was now a force to be reckoned with.

CHAPTER SEVENTEEN

New York, NY

"You can't always write a chord ugly enough to say what you want to say, so sometimes you have to rely on a giraffe filled with whipped cream."

~ Frank Zappa

And Then The Call Came...

At the end of April 1967 I was in Pomona, California finishing my sophomore year in college when Frank called me from New York and said, "Hey, do you want to come work for me this summer?"

He was a month into the "Absolutely Freee"—yes, that's spelled correctly—show that he and the Mothers were doing at the 200-seat Garrick Theater.

The Garrick, owned by Howard and Elly Solomon, was on Bleecker Street in Greenwich Village.

It was above the Cafe Au-Go-Go. Frank and the Mothers were the first rock artists to play at the Garrick.

I asked Frank what he wanted me to do and he said, "I need someone reliable to buy me cigarettes and coffee."

I figured that was his way of saying he really didn't have a job description for me yet but if I came, he'd think of a job for me.

He said. "Look, if you're interested, I want to see if you can handle the music business and maybe end up working for me full-time."

"That sounds like a plan," I said. "Hey, can you use any additional help, like maybe a roadie or two?" Frank said, "Who'd you have in mind?"

I mentioned my friends Bill Harris and Dick Barber, whom Frank knew from our days in Claremont in the early 1960s.

Bill Harris, Dick Barber and Bobby at LAX before Bob's flight to Australia.

Bill, Dick, and I went to Claremont High School together and have been friends ever since. Frank said to tell them that he couldn't guarantee long-term employment but if they were willing to give it a try then they should make the trip.

When I finished my sophomore year in college that June, Bill, Dick, and I set out for New York in a friend's VW Beetle.

The friend, someone Dick knew, had moved to Connecticut and needed her car driven from California to the east coast. She agreed to pay for gas and we agreed not to trash her car.

We left L.A. early one morning in mid-June with little money and unrealistic expectations. Marcia knew that I had to explore this opportunity with Frank and since it was summer and I wasn't in school, she smiled and waved as we headed out to seek our destiny.

It took us five days to drive across the country. It reminded me of the first cross-country trip our family took when we left Edgewood, Maryland. But this ride had beer and was a lot more fun.

We took Route 66 like Dad did when the family made our way west and stayed in cheap motels along the way. Bill, Dick and I stayed at similar places and chowed down in cheap fast food joints, which hadn't existed in the 1950s.

Our road trip gave us each the chance to think about what might be possible as musical hangers-on and how we'd handle those opportunities.

I told Bill and Dick that I was sure we'd end up working for Frank in an important capacity and that we would make big bucks.

Bill was skeptical and Dick thought I was delusional. I let them have their doubts, but I knew we were in for a transformative adventure.

Dick Barber is one of those guys that other men envy. He is a master mechanic, knows engines, transmissions, and electronics. He even built and now flies his own airplane. He's the kind of rock steady, hyper-rational, and technically proficient person that Frank needed in his entourage.

In fact, Frank asked Dick to be his first road manager for the Mothers, a job that lasted many years for Dick and proved my original prediction that he could be a great asset.

Bill Harris was our high school senior class president who then graduated from Claremont

McKenna College, one of the schools in the Claremont Colleges consortium.

He still has a brilliant sense of humor and is a superb writer and lecturer. He worked in a series of clerical jobs in Pomona before deciding to give show business a try.

It was clear from the start that he had a future in the entertainment industry, but as fate would have it, just not with Frank and the Mothers of Invention. After almost 54 years I am still in close touch with Bill and Dick.

Of the three of us, Dick was the best equipped to handle the technical parts of our trip. He was the best driver and knew how to read a road map (I knew how to read a topographical map from my days as a Marine, but that wasn't much help).

It was also Dick's friend's car we were using. After 3,000 miles of navigating America's interstate highways it was he who bravely headed down the helix, the circuitously winding road that leads to the entrance of the Lincoln Tunnel.

We then went under the Hudson River and then exited onto the wildly congested streets of Manhattan.

As we approached the exit for the Lincoln Tunnel, the sight of the New York skyline was overwhelming.

Downtown L.A. is a sprawling, disconnected city that closes down at the end of each workday.

But New York is not L.A. It's alive 24/7. It's the Big Apple, Frank Sinatra's "city that never sleeps." For three Southern California boys it was the equivalent of landing on Neptune.

It was scary and exhilarating and Bill and I sat in awed silence as Dick maneuvered into uncharted territory.

It was a typical New York summer day: the smell of hot asphalt, humidity, and mixed food aromas filled the air. Dick patiently drove through the sluggish traffic until we found the Garrick Theater on Bleecker Street near Frank's apartment.

He found a parking spot on a side street, maneuvered the car into place, and we went looking for Frank's apartment. We found the building on Thompson Street. It was a modest structure that looked like it was built in the 1930s.

I pushed the intercom buzzer and a woman answered. I told her who I was and that we had just arrived from California. She said, "Frank is still asleep." I looked at my watch; it was 4:00 p.m.

"You'll have to come back later," she said, which was not much of a welcome.

I came to appreciate Frank's nocturnal work habits after seeing him play two performances a night, then stay up afterwards coming down from the adrenaline rush of his shows. We decided to get something to eat before trying to see him later.

We walked around the corner to the Bitter End Cafe on Bleecker Street, where acts like George Carlin, Bob Dylan, and Peter, Paul and Mary had performed. It opened in 1962 and in 1967 it still had some of the hottest acts of the day.

The industrial strength air conditioning gave us relief from the afternoon heat and we ordered hamburgers, fries, and beer.

We stared at photos of musicians and comedians and basked in this new, celebrity-laden atmosphere.

The waitress brought our burgers along with the check. Our meal came to $15, which would be a bargain now, 50 years later, but it was a lot of money in 1967 for three not-yet-employed guys.

It's no wonder there were so many skinny, malnourished people in the Village. They couldn't afford to eat and it looked like we were going to have the same problem.

In a mild state of shock, we ate our pricey burgers and fries and drank the overpriced beer.

An hour and a half later, we wondered whether or not this great adventure was going to work out. We left the Cafe and went back to Frank's apartment.

This time Frank answered with a big, "Hi!" and buzzed the lock on the street level door to let us in. The elevator barely held the three of us and had the odor of cat piss.

The stairwells were grimy and littered with candy wrappers, cigarette butts, and other debris. Frank's floor had one light at each end of the hallway. It was depressing and dismal, not a great advertisement for New York City living.

Frank answered our knock on the door, let out a laugh, and said, "Welcome to New York!" He asked if we wanted anything to drink. We said no and told him about the meal at the Bitter End.

He shook his head and smiled, "Don't worry, there's a much better and cheaper place to eat on the next block called The Trio. It's run by a Greek family." I filed that as a mental note.

There's No Business...

Frank was barefoot and shirtless and thinner than I had ever seen him. He looked haggard, which I could tell was from lack of sleep. His apartment was sweltering and smelled of stale coffee and cigarette butts.

There was only a window unit blowing a puny puff of cool air. His place reminded me of Ralph Cramden's apartment in "The Honeymooners."

Frank said, "You can start work by coming to the show and you'll stay at Calvin Shenkle's apartment for tonight."

Calvin was Frank's album cover artist-in-residence who designed some of the most memorable covers from Frank's enormous songbook.

"And after that?" I asked.

Frank said, "I'll figure that out. In the meantime, get your stuff and drop it off at Calvin's."

"Can't we just leave it in the car overnight?" I asked. Frank said, "No way. It's not safe."

As we were leaving for Calvin's with our suitcases Frank said, "Be careful with your car, the cops like to tow illegally parked cars."

Not paying much attention to his advice, I switched gears and asked him, "So what is it you're going to need us to do?"

"I'll figure out what Bill and Dick can do when you get back here," Frank said. "But for now I just want you to hang out with me and go where I go, capeesh?"

At the time, that made me feel pretty fucking important. But when he'd first invited me to come and said he wanted me to buy him cigarettes and coffee, I hadn't realized he meant that literally.

I didn't know yet how awkward I was going to feel about being paid to just hang out with Frank and basically do nothing but get him cigarettes and coffee. Clearly, it wasn't going to be a steep learning curve.

With Dick once again driving we rode around until we found Calvin's apartment in Hell's Kitchen, an area in midtown Manhattan between 34th and 59th streets on the west side of the island. Calvin's place was on 49th street. In those days, Hell's Kitchen was about as nice as its name implied.

Today it's been rebuilt with skyscraper offices, trendy and ultra-expensive condominiums and apartment rentals, and equally trendy restaurants. Hell's Kitchen is now Heck's Butler's Pantry.

Dick miraculously found another parking spot and we went up to Calvin's apartment lugging our belongings. The one bit of Frank's advice we did pay attention to was to not leave anything of value in the car, especially in the neighborhood where Calvin lived.

Frank had let Calvin know ahead of time that we were coming so he was waiting for us when we rang his bell.

Although not a member of the band, Calvin was indistinguishable from the image the group projected: long hair, hippie clothes, gaunt. In the Marines it was called the uniform of the day.

He was incredibly nice to us, and we appreciated his welcoming attitude. After leaving Frank I wouldn't see Calvin again until 2012 when we were asked to appear together on a PBS show called, "History Detectives."

We were asked to verify a painting that was supposed to have been painted by Frank and that had been purchased at a thrift store somewhere in the south for only $5. It turned out to be one that Frank had, in fact, painted and was then valued at over $25,000.

Anyway, Calvin's apartment wasn't much better or bigger than Frank's. It had just enough floor space for the three of us to crash. We didn't have much time to settle in or rest because the first show started at 9:00 p.m. and we wanted to be there plenty early to see everything there was to see.

Having been to quite a few of Frank's shows in California, I wasn't sure what to expect from such a small venue. Up to that point my only recollections of watching Frank perform were based on his shows in large auditoriums.

I had no frame of reference for how the band would do their mayhem in the small theater environment. It was something I was anxious to see and experience.

The Garrick Theater had only 200 seats but they were filled for both shows almost every night the Mothers performed. I was nervous on my first night in show business.

I wasn't sure of my role yet and my hair wasn't long enough and none of my clothes had a floral pattern. Bill and Dick were shorthaired and flower-less, too.

We looked exactly like what we were: three out of place California dudes. After splashing water on our faces we set out for our first night with the Mothers. We arrived at the Garrick by 8:00 p.m., nervous, anxious, and out of place.

CHAPTER EIGHTEEN

Absolutely Marvelous

"Art is making something out of nothing and selling it."

~ **Frank Zappa**

Absolutely Freee

The first "Absolutely Freee" show we saw that night was filled with manic energy, crisp sound quality, and the kind of antics that the Mothers were becoming famous for.

Jimmy Carl Black, Roy Estrada, and Frank danced and moved about on stage, both in unison and individually, creating a visually comedic touch to the body-rumbling, brain-rattling volume.

The Mothers of Invention were in rare form. Billy Mundi, Don Preston, and Bunk Gardner played like they were performing at Carnegie Hall.

The seamlessness of their interaction with Frank was stunning and the audience loved every minute. It was the best time I'd ever had with Frank and the band and I couldn't wait to go to work for him.

The prospect of being associated with that much creativity, enthusiasm, sarcasm, musical talent, and honest-to-goodness brilliance was exciting.

By comparison, very few of the other emerging rock bands of that era had the same audience attention-grabbing devices. Watching Frank and the Mothers perform was almost like a kind of therapy.

You would go into the theater expecting to hear loud music but then be given the added opportunity to lose yourself in the uplifting and humorous psychodrama that was the band's trademark.

Anyone reading this who went to one or more of those shows will understand what I'm trying to describe. "Absolutely Freee" was a microcosm of the amazing musical intricacies that Frank composed, coupled with the pure enjoyment of watching hairy young men make fools of themselves.

Those shows were the best entertainment value in the rock genre of the day and they helped to establish Frank's image as a master showman and audience provocateur. At 2:00 a.m., after the last show, we went back to Calvin's apartment and gave in to our exhaustion.

The next morning we awoke to find that our car had been towed. There were parking spaces alright, but nobody told us they were used by New York City traffic cops to trap unsuspecting tourists.

Anyone who has had their car towed in New York City is certain that the traffic gremlins put up mixed message and confusing signs in order to intentionally snare drivers.

And even if we had seen one or more of those signs, we were certainly not capable of understanding what they meant at that hour. After a few calls to the NYPD, we found out where to retrieve the car. The three of us took a taxi to the west side dock where the infamous car pound is located.

When we got to the window to pay, the graffiti scratched on the wall read: "Don't feel bad. They got Trini Lopez, too."

We felt much better after seeing that. Fortunately, Frank had given us $50, which was what it cost in those days to liberate your car from the clutches of the NYPD traffic authority.

That afternoon, Dick's friend, the car owner, came down on a bus from Connecticut. Dick met her at the Port Authority parking lot where he handed over the keys to her recently impounded car.

He thought it best not to mention the impound. She gave Dick a ride back to the Garrick and then she headed back to Connecticut. Being California car guys, we were now without wheels and felt trapped. How were we going to make our getaway if we wanted to split?

We realized that part of our plan had not been well thought out. Anxiety set in.

The next night the shows were even better. The band played Call Any Vegetable, Big Dilemma about my

Big Leg Emma, and several other songs that would appear on the "Ruben and the Jets" album.

Before the show Frank told me to look for two teenage boys who had been there the night before for both shows. He said to let them in for free.

Frank nicknamed them Leopold and Loeb because they were wealthy, not because they'd kidnapped or murdered anybody.

They were just two Jewish kids from Long Island who had been coming to the Garrick to see the Mothers of Invention since the show opened.

They continued to come at least three times a week until the show closed in September. Their status as "super fans" earned them their free seats.

They brought bags of fruit, vegetables, cookies, and soda, which the band would either consume before the show or use for stage props. On any given night Jimmy Carl might put a handful of kale in his open fly along with a banana.

Or Roy would grab two grapefruits and stuffed them up under his shirt and then hold Oreo cookies in front of each one. Their use of fruits and vegetables was delightfully absurd improvisation and it changed every night.

During his time at the Garrick, Frank came to know Jimi Hendrix. They met in July of 1967 after Jimi returned to New York from the Monterey International Pop Festival.

Some of Jimi's band members went to hear Miles Davis and Dizzy Gillespie one night at Village Gate jazz club down the street from the Garrick. Jimi went to the Garrick to see the Mothers of Invention.

After the show, Jimi, along with his drummer Buddy Miles, went to Frank's new apartment on Charles Street near Seventh Avenue in the Village.

Frank told me about the time Jimi and Buddy came to his apartment. Buddy came in, sat down on the sofa, and immediately fell asleep. Frank and Jimi talked about music and guitars.

When Jimi was ready to leave Frank said he bent over and his ball squeezer bellbottoms split at the seam and he had to have them stitched up before he could leave.

A few weeks later, The Mothers of Invention recorded "We're Only in It for the Money." The "Absolutely Freee" show was becoming a cultural phenomenon in the Village. The band played two shows each night, six nights a week. During those shows anything might happen.

The New York Times journalist and music critic Dan Sullivan even gave it a good review on May 25, 1967. In short, Sullivan said that… "Frank's work was pure genius."

Those shows were a magical mix of sights and sounds, the forerunners of other shows the band would do on tour and the kind of audience-grabbing performances that other groups tried to imitate, but with nowhere near the same intensity or humor.

One evening Dick Barber and I went out to Long Island to deliver some sound equipment that needed to be repaired. We found out later that while we were gone four Marines in their dress blue uniforms came into the Garrick.

Frank had them come up on stage and pretend to mutilate rubber dolls. The audience was stunned as the Marines mimed killing the dolls while the Mothers played furiously behind them.

A black Marine at the front of the group had just come home from Vietnam. He broke down in tears and shouted, "Eat the apple and fuck the Corps!"

I knew that phrase from my time in the Marines. It's one of those military expressions that made little sense, unless you were a Marine. It was sometimes used during stressful or dangerous combat conditions.

The audience probably just went along thinking, "Far out, man." When the Marines were done letting off steam, they walked out of the theater into the crowd that always gathered on Bleecker Street. Frank never saw them again.

At some shows you might see audience members come up on stage and act on impulses, like spontaneously singing with the band or removing articles of clothing, neither of which were discouraged.

That kind of audience participation got passed around by word of mouth (the early form of social media), which kept people coming back for more.

In addition to the Garrick where Frank was playing, Linda Ronstadt and the Stone Poneys were playing in the Cafe Au-Go-Go, another part of the building owned by Howard Solomon.

Billy Mundi sometimes played drums for Linda when he wasn't playing with the Mothers.

Before the Stone Poneys, a group called the Fugs with Ed Sanders, Tuli Kupferberg, Steve Taylor, Coby Batty, and Steve Petito sometimes performed at Cafe Au-Go-Go.

They shared billing with Danny Kalb, Al Kooper and the Blues Project, the Jim Kweskin Jug Band, and Richie Havens.

Frank wanted to produce an album for Richie but there was a disagreement about the title of the album. Frank wanted to call it "The Mad Gummer" because Richie was missing his whole top row of teeth. Cal Schenkle even designed the album cover showing a cut-away of Richie's jaw without teeth.

But Richie didn't think that was how he wanted to be known to his audience so, sadly, the project never got off the ground. Luckily, after Richie was such a huge hit at Woodstock, and became a frequent guest on "The Tonight Show" with Johnny Carson, Johnny talked Richie into getting dental implants.

Linda Ronstadt and Frank had the same manager, an intense and compact man named Herbie Cohen. Herbie was one of those show biz characters that you read about.

He was tough, funny, and loved by everyone except those he did business with. They usually ended up suing him.

Herbie was born in the South Bronx, served in the Marine Corps, and worked for a time as a fireman. He began his career in the music business in the folk-music scene, running nightclubs including Cosmo Alley, where Lenny Bruce performed his controversial comedy act laced with the then forbidden "dirty words."

Lenny's arrest for obscenities was the inspiration for George Carlin's "seven dirty words"—shit, piss, fuck, cunt, cocksucker, motherfucker, and tits.

Maybe Carlin's use of profanity led my brother to his later fight for the freedom of speech in the Senate hearings on the Parent's Resource Music Center (PMRC).

Herbie Cohen was also known for keeping a pistol under the bar in his clubs. Another colorful rumor about his unorthodox business style was that he kept a box of hand-grenades in his car.

I'm not sure if any of the rumors about him were true but he was certainly one of the flower-power music scene's most interesting characters.

In the late 50s, another rumor that added to his colorful persona was that he had gone to South Africa as a mercenary, supplying arms for the Congolese revolutionary leader Patrice Lumumba.

A Jewish music mogul, Marine, mercenary and gunrunner: the perfect qualities for a manager of artistic talent.

Cohen went on to manage my brother who once described him as "a little Jewish man that nobody likes who always wears nylon shirts."

Cohen also managed Captain Beefheart and Tim Buckley. With his brother and attorney, "Mutt"

Cohen, Herbie set up the record labels Straight and Bizarre.

Frank told me the story about Herbie having been a mercenary. I also heard somewhere that Herbie was an accountant. I knew him from how he did business.

Herbie and the owner of the Garrick and Cafe Au-Go-Go, Howard Solomon, were having a heated discussion one night about the evening's gate.

I was there waiting to take the money from that night's shows over to the Manufacturer's Hanover Bank night drop box.

Herbie paid two New York City cops $25 each per week to escort me nightly to the drop box. That was my most responsible assignment and I took it very seriously.

I never knew how much money was in the night drop bag but I was glad I had two armed NYPD cops with me when I went to the bank. The cops were waiting upstairs while Herbie, Howard, and I were downstairs.

Herbie and Howard were in each other's faces and it didn't look like either was going to give in. Howard opened his briefcase and pulled out a knife.

Herbie drew a small hatchet from his desk drawer. Here were two middle-aged Jewish men in the basement of a New York music club, weapons drawn, and arguing over money.

I figured this was how people in New York did business. I sat back and watched the show. Herbie and Howard were arguing intently about how many tickets were sold when one of the cops stuck his head in the door and asked when we would be going to the night drop.

The presence of law enforcement was enough for both men to back down. Herbie gave me the moneybag and I left with the cops.

The next day I saw Herbie and Howard having coffee together in a cafe on Bleecker Street like they were best buddies.

My first lesson in show business: nothing is as it appears, especially when money is involved.

Man on the street

One day Frank asked me to go with him to the CBS building at 52nd Street and Sixth Avenue across from the New York Hilton.

He had a meeting with a record company executive. At 11:00 a.m. we walked over to Sixth Avenue, flagged a taxi and headed uptown.

By 49th Street the traffic was at a standstill and the meter was running, so we got out and walked the remaining three blocks to CBS.

As we crossed 51st Street I saw a large man with long grey hair and beard. He was wearing what looked like a bearskin coat and a helmet with horns.

He was holding a staff and a tin cup, and sporting sunglasses.

I couldn't imagine how he was able to stand the heat in that getup but he seemed perfectly comfortable. Frank walked up to him and put a five-dollar bill in his cup.

The man said, "Thanks, Frank," and Frank replied, "What's happening, Moondog?"

Frank had not said a word to the man before giving him money. The man was obviously blind yet somehow he knew it was Frank.

I wondered how. I thought maybe his sense of smell was stronger than mine, like a dog can smell someone he knows.

I, on the other hand, noticed no aroma emanating from my brother, nor from Moondog, although he looked as if it had been quite some time since he'd taken a bath.

Moondog was a fixture on Sixth Avenue. His real name was Louis Thomas Hardin and he was born in 1916 in Marysville, Kansas.

He lost his sight at age 13 when he was standing near a dynamite cap when it exploded. He learned to play the violin, viola, piano, and organ when he went to The Iowa School for the Blind.

In 1933 he went to The Missouri School for the Blind where he studied Braille. He came to New York in 1943 and worked as a model for art students.

He also panhandled on the streets to supplement his meager income. He adopted the name Moondog in honor of a dog that used to howl at the moon. He died in 1999 at the age of 83.

That he and Frank knew each other didn't surprise me; they were both musicians and under other circumstances their roles could have easily been reversed. Remember Frank's Pacific Grove exploding bomb mishap?

Cafeteria Manners

It was another blistering summer day, so Frank and I were wearing T-shirts. He had on tight bellbottoms and I was wearing baggy shorts.

When we got into the building I figured our casual outfits would draw no second glances since they'd expect Frank to look like a hippie musician, not a CBS corporate exec.

We were headed to a record company that made millions of dollars off of musicians who didn't dress any better than Frankie and me.

Except for the massive power outage in 1965, New York City in the latter half of the 1960s didn't have many problems with blackouts and brownouts. In those days, when the A/C was working, it was so freezing cold that you could almost see your breath.

We walked into the CBS building and were immediately hit with a blast of cold that gave my bare legs a chill. Frank walked over to the directory, found the floor of the person he was going to see, and we headed to the elevators.

We rode up to the 18th floor. The receptionist was a large black woman who greeted us with a smile and no apparent judgment regarding our casual appearance. Frank gave his name and said we had an appointment.

She asked us to have a seat and picked up the phone to announce our arrival. After a few seconds she told us to go down the corridor and into the record executive's office.

I told Frank that I'd wait there in the office lobby. I was always intimidated by the business dealings Frank had with music industry people, Herbie included. I felt less anxious sitting by myself trying to look cool, instead of just cold.

As I leafed through magazines I began wondering why I was there. I knew so little about the music business and had no musical talent whatsoever.

I knew I would never be in the band and I was beginning to have second, third, and fourth thoughts about my future with Frank. I relished my role as my brother's protector, but that wasn't an official title.

As a Marine I guess I was tough enough, but I didn't have the build to join the ranks of heavy weight bodyguards he needed over the course of his career, which included a few NYPD cops, and everybody's favorite, John Smothers.

John was a very large, bald, black man who wore his judogi, the traditional judo uniform, when he was guarding Frank.

And woe be it for anyone stupid enough to try to get close to Frank when Smothers was around. He could turn into one scary dude.

Frank returned and said, "Let's go to the cafeteria. My meeting got pushed back an hour."

We took the elevator down to the CBS cafeteria and walked into a big room full of tables, chairs, and a long serving counter. We got in line and started shuffling along with CBS employees.

I was ahead of Frank, putting food on my tray when I heard my brother yell, "What the fuck are you talking about?"

When I turned around I saw Frank standing toe-to-toe with a tall balding man in a tan Brooks Brothers summer suit. The man took a threatening pose, and looked like he was going to punch Frank.

Frank calmly took a step back, extended his arms with the tray in his hands, and dropped the tray full of food onto the guy's shoes.

Frank said to me, "C'mon, let's get the fuck out of here."

He turned and walked out of the cafeteria. I hurried after him, but not before putting a sandwich in my pocket. The guy was screaming "ASSHOLE!" but my brother never flinched nor even turned around.

I, on the other hand, looked back to see Mr. Brooks Brothers Suit bending down to wipe food off his shoes and pants.

I was nervous the incident might affect Frank's relationship with CBS. Frank, on the other hand, didn't seem to have even the slightest bit of concern.

We went back down to the street level. Frank was stone cold silent, and my brother was nobody to fuck with when he was angry. I didn't even ask what Mr. Brooks Brothers had said. When Frank was in a mood like that there was no talking to him.

I figured he'd tell me when he calmed down. Instead I took the wrapper off my sandwich and began to eat. We walked out to Sixth Avenue and hailed a cab.

We were nearly back down to the Village when Frank turned to me and said, "That son of a bitch said I looked like a faggot."

I looked at Frank, smiled, and said, "Nice job with the tray." Frank smiled back. Needless to say, Frank missed his appointment but my worries had been in vain. That never seemed to affect his career any.

Bohacks and The West Village

After a week of sleeping on the floor in Calvin's apartment, Frank found a sublet for Dick, Bill, and me in the West Village. Dick was getting more involved with various roadie tasks and his hours were more erratic than ours so he decided to stay with Calvin.

That was a good thing because the new apartment was only a one-bedroom and would've been a tight squeeze for three guys.

Luckily, after two years of college and a series of part-time jobs to help pay for my classes, I had lost enough weight so that I didn't take up extra space anymore.

I hadn't yet achieved the Greenwich Village skinny hippie look, but I was a lot thinner. Our new digs were in the heart of the West Village, above a market named Bohack's.

It was across from Sheridan Square on Washington Place and Barrow Street. The building even had a doorman, an amenity that Frank's new building did not have.

Frank felt obligated to take care of us, but not for too long. The sublet was only for four weeks. He figured that was enough time for us to decide if we wanted to continue working for him.

There was no shortage of things to amuse us in the Village. Sheridan Square was in perpetual motion after dark.

There were clubs we walked past after the Garrick closed for the night but because we didn't have enough money to go into them we stood in front watching people who did. That was a good show in itself.

A disco paradise called "Salvation" was co-owned by Jerry Schatzberg, Faye Dunaway's then-boyfriend. He co-owned it with a guy named Bradley Pierce.

If you could afford to get in you'd see people like Liza Minelli, Mia Farrow, Jim Morrison, and members of The Yardbirds.

Bill and I frequently stood outside Salvation and watched for celebrities until we realized that this behavior fell under the get-a-life heading for us.

It didn't take long for Dick Barber to establish himself as a valuable asset to Frank and the band. His vast technical knowledge and mechanical skills were exceeded only by his calm, professional disposition. Frank realized that about Dick early in our time with him.

Bill and I, on the other hand, weren't fitting into The Mother's organizational structure.

Buying cigarettes and coffee was not a career path for either of us. By the end of August, I told Frank that we would be going home.

It was difficult for me to tell him I was leaving because I felt that I had let him down and that I had wasted his time. I watched his face to see how he would react. He could have gotten pissed off or simply disgusted, but he didn't do either of those things.

He looked at me for a long few seconds and then said: "Look Bobby, I'm sorry that it didn't work out but I'm glad you gave it a try. I think you need that diploma because Dad will be happy at least one of us got an education." Then he laughed in a way that expressed his disdain for formal education.

He had Herbie buy Bill and me tickets on an American Airlines flight from JFK back to LAX. Our foray into the world of rock and roll was coming to a close. Frank thanked Bill for giving it a try and wished him well in his other career goals.

Bill and I were both down in the dumps after that, but we knew we had to go. Dick returned to California but a few weeks later was called back by Frank to become the band's first road manager for another one of their European tours in 1969.

Bill moved to L.A. where he got a job at ABC Television writing for gossip columnist and TV personality Rona Barrett. I went back to college.

It felt disorienting coming back to suburban California and the routine of classes at my university. Did I make a big mistake? Did I give up too soon? When I was back on campus I had the ominous feeling that whatever I ended up doing would never be as exciting, unpredictable or glamorous as the rock and roll business.

On the other hand, the financial uncertainty of working in a non-performing role in the music business was just too tenuous for me.

I needed more structure, more order in my life. Besides, my hair would never be long enough, I didn't like ball squeezer bell-bottoms, and shirts with flowers on them gave me the willies.

So I ended up making peace with my decision but I still had a nagging feeling that I was leaving my brother just as he was on the verge of becoming a major star in the highly competitive and, as it turned out, very dangerous world of rock and roll.

I knew I would be missing out on being with Frank during his rapidly accelerating rise as a performer and deep thinker, but I had to face the fact that I had developed a more traditional value system than the hippie culture when it came to dealing with men and women of that era.

Some of the women I met during that time were, to put it mildly, tough. I never got used to that. Having been an active duty Marine, trying to fit into the hippie culture of the 1960s was just not in me.

After I had left Frank in New York City, his show, "Absolutely Freee," ran until September 5, 1967. Not long after the show closed, Frank and the Mothers left for their first European tour.

On September 23, 1967, they played their first concert at the Royal Albert Hall in London.

As events unfolded in Frank's career, I regretted leaving him and wished I'd been by his side during that horrible December in 1971.

First, a fan's flare set off a raging fire in Montreux. It was the event that inspired Deep Purple's hit song, "Smoke on the Water."

The whole theater burned down and Frank's band lost all of its difficult-to-replace customized equipment.

Second, I also felt helpless when, two weeks later at a London show, a drug-addled audience member, Trevor Howell, pushed Frank off the stage and sent him down 15 feet into the orchestra pit and nearly killed him.

The attack cut his chin, created a hole in the back of his head, broke a rib, and fractured his leg. One arm was paralyzed and his larynx was crushed forcing the pitch of his voice to drop a third.

I was full of rage about that incident and felt enormous guilt that I'd left him to deal with something like that alone. I will never know if I could have helped him in either instance, but that those things happened to Frank when I wasn't there for him, made me furious.

CHAPTER NINETEEN

Stockholm, Sweden

"Let's not be too rough on our own ignorance; it's what makes America great!"

~ Frank Zappa

Higher Education Abroad

After leaving Frank in 1967, I went back to college full-time, while Marcia started working at Pacific State, a psychiatric hospital not far from where I was attending college.

With each course I took, every paper I wrote, or test I stumbled through, I realized that time was going by faster than it had at any other point in my life.

In June of 1969 I graduated and received my college diploma, the only original Zappa family member, other than our father, to do so. In August of 1969

Marcia and I packed our belongings and put them in a friend's garage in L.A.

I had been accepted to graduate school for social psychology at the University of Stockholm in Sweden. After college, I wanted to travel, to see more of the world than I had when I was in the Marine Corps. And I wanted to see it under more pleasant conditions.

We were about to make a big move. Well, not big for me as Frank and I had spent our entire lives moving from place to place. This move, though, was of my own doing, which I was quite excited about.

This was the era when college graduates could, if they had the money, take time after college to go to Europe and soak up Western Civilization culture, drink some really good beer, and try not to create an international incident involving a U.S. Embassy rescue mission.

I told Frank what I was going to do and he said, "That sounds pretty interesting, Bobby. Just don't get into any trouble." But Stockholm wasn't Tijuana, so I was confident I could stay out of jail.

Marcia and I flew out of San Francisco and landed at the Arlanda airport outside Stockholm. We collected our bags, got on a bus and checked into a Stockholm motel.

The enormity of what we were about to do was sinking in. First we had to find a place to live. Then learn enough of the language to function day-to-day.

The average Swede spoke two or three languages, English often being one of them. Common courtesy dictated that as foreign guests in Sweden we learn at least the language basics when shopping in liquor stores or a Stockholm version of bodegas.

We also had to figure out how to get around the city and live within the meager budget we had set aside for the year from student loans and yard sale money.

By 1969 Frank Zappa and the Mothers had become established as one of the most avant-garde rock groups in the world. They were playing all over the U.S. and throughout Europe. My big brother Frankie was now famous.

One day, while walking in downtown Stockholm's center city, Marcia and I passed a record store. There in the window was the poster of Frank sitting on the toilet with his pants down around his ankles looking out at the world.

Over the next nine months I came across that poster in England, Ireland, Finland, and all around Sweden. I loved seeing that poster and watching as young, shaggy-haired kids saw it, laughed, and bought it.

Frank told me that he was paid $1,500 to pose for that poster. The guy who reproduced it made many times more. Frank was now an internationally recognized figure, and not just for his zany poses.

His music was becoming an underground phenomenon. Underground because we never heard him on the radio but whenever he played in person his shows were sold out within hours.

Yes, changes were in the air. I was now a full-time graduate student. Frank was now a full-time musician. Both of us were doing what we were supposed to be doing.

We had risen above our dysfunctional family background and somehow stayed sane in spite of all the manic moving.

The Nobel Prize in Economics

In December of 1969 the head of the sociology department at the University of Stockholm told a number of students that he had 12 tickets to the first Nobel ceremony for the Economics prize to be held at the Konserthuset, the Swedish music hall.

He asked if any of us wanted to go. I jumped at the opportunity and on the night of Wednesday, December 10, 1969 Marcia and I, with 10 other students, went to the Nobel award ceremony.

The Stockholm Concert Hall, or as it's known to the Swedes, the Stockholms Konserthus / Kungliga Filharmonikerna, or simply Konserthuset, is home to the Stockholm Philharmonic Orchestra.

The Nobel Prize awards ceremony is now held there every year. The Konserthuset opened in 1926 and has long been a cultural statement in the city's landscape, revered for its architecture and statuary by Carl Milles, whose sculpture "Fountain of the Muses" was at New York's Metropolitan Museum for 20 years.

The stage is reminiscent of the acoustically perfect Carnegie Hall stage and the interior is old world elegant. The front of the building has ten enormous columns and when lit in the evening the façade shines a dazzling shade of blue.

That night we sat in the balcony of the Konserthuset and watched as the Nobel Prize winners received their award from King Carl Gustav XVI of Sweden. It was one of the most inspiring and humbling experiences I had ever had.

The pomp and circumstance were fascinating. It occurred to me that we were witnessing a piece of history in one of Sweden's most important public buildings.

The Nobel Prize in Economics that year went to M.I.T. Professor Paul Samuelson, who I would meet a few years later when I worked for McGraw-Hill Publishing. Dr. Samuelson was the author of one of the most successful textbooks in economics ever published.

What made the Konserthuset even more special was that it was the same venue that Frank and the Mothers had played two years earlier. I was amused to be sitting in this building watching this glorious ceremony knowing that my brother had played there, too.

As I watched the Nobel ceremonies I couldn't help but marvel about the stark contrast between this presentation versus a performance given by my wild, pushing-the-limits brother and his band.

I knew that what Frank and the Mothers must've done on this stage was the polar opposite of the high-class performance I was watching then.

Playing for the home crowd

In June of 1970, after graduate school, Marcia and I came back to Los Angeles. Ronald Reagan was governor and an economic recession of epic proportions was underway. Jobs were scarce and the future was bleak.

Marcia was pregnant with our son, Jason, and I needed to find work to get us reestablished.

I kept plugging away until I found a job refinancing loans and collecting past due accounts with a finance company. The long swim upward was beginning. Meanwhile, the Mothers were scheduled to do a show in Minneapolis before going back out on the road for another European tour. Before the Mothers left for their next European tour they did one show in Santa Monica that summer.

Frank always took time for the fans – even the young ones.

I wasn't so much interested in seeing that show, mainly because I needed to get back to our apartment to help Marcia, but I did want to see Frank.

I was standing in the crowd outside of the auditorium at the Santa Monica pier when Frank pulled up in a limo. He got out and the fans went crazy yelling. He ignored them, reached into his back pocket, and pulled out his wallet.

The limo driver had gotten out and was holding the door for Frank. Frank pulled out a wad of bills and handed them to the driver. Frank wasn't obsessed with fame and I think he wanted to show that you have to pay people for what they do. It was a gesture that fans recognized as pure Frank Zappa: no pretense, no bullshit.

I caught Frank's attention, waved, and he came over. He gave me a big grin and a hug. We talked briefly before the show. He asked how I was and if I was working and I told him about my job working for the finance company and collecting bills.

He shook his head and said: "You'd better get your shit together and get away from that bullshit." That was, as we both knew, a firm grasp of the obvious. But he had to say it, I guess. I was concerned by how tired he looked but glad to see he was in great spirits.

He loved performing and traveling and his fans loved him. The rest of his tour and my own busy schedule kept us from seeing each other again until that October.

*Jason with his Uncle Frank in Frankie's basement on
Woodrow Wilson Drive.*

When LIFE was hot

Things were coming together for Frank. He was
getting recognized worldwide for his music. He was
recording albums, writing music, touring, doing
interviews for TV, radio, and print, and working on a
movie. On the cover of the September 24, 1971 issue of
LIFE Magazine was a picture of the Jackson Five.

The lead article was "Rock Stars at Home with
Their Parents." On pages 46 and 47 was a two-page, four
color spread showing Frank with Mom and Dad. Our
parents were seated on the couch and Frank was
standing in front of them holding a cat.

I still have two copies of the original LIFE Magazine with that picture in it. My brother, mother, and father were together for one brief moment of fame. I thought it was interesting, though, that the article focused on rock musicians' nuclear families. I guess the idea was to show the genesis of each artist's talent, if that was possible.

Frank was in great company in that issue. Other pieces on parents with musicians included Elton John, Eric Clapton, The Jackson Five, Ginger Baker, Joe Cocker, Grace Slick, David Crosby, and Richie Havens. The stories were about these rock stars and how proud their parents were of what their kids had accomplished.

Frank said our parent's comments in the article said a lot about their perception of him at that point in his life. He said that he always felt that Mom and Dad had a very dull existence and that was his motivation for experiencing so many other things in his own life, especially music.

Dad said that since he played guitar in college he thought that might have influenced Frank to pursue a career in music. But Dad could not have foreseen how far Frank would take his own musical talent well beyond any influence Dad may have had on him.

In his retirement, Dad thought about going into acting. He thought he had the looks and the experience of age in his favor. He just didn't have any acting skills. Frank's attitude toward Dad's acting ambition was tinged with sarcasm after all the years of Dad's disdain for Frank's musical interests.

Mom was more practical in her observation about Frank. She said that she was envious of Frank because: "…his hair is curlier than mine – and blacker."

My impression of the image the three of them conveyed is of proud parents, especially Mom, and a rather blasé son who did the article to please Mom and Dad but that he couldn't wait for it to be over so he could get back to his music.

Frank told me later that our parent's quotes were edited to make them sound as normal as anybody's mom and dad. He didn't specify what was edited but I suspect it was something Dad said that would have given the impression that Frank's talent was due, in part, to his influence as a father.

In one of the photographs used for Frank's story you can see an oil painting on the wall that hung in Frank's house. Edward Beardsley, a professor at the

University of California at Riverside and one of Frank's and my close friends from our days in Claremont, had painted it.

Professor Beardsley painted two pictures with the same character, a heavyset man with a mustache holding a cup of coffee. Frank had one and I have the other. This one's mine, it's called "Suburban Sunrise:"

"Suburban Sunrise" by Professor Edward Beardsley

CHAPTER TWENTY

Los Angeles, CA

"Music is always a commentary on society."

-    **Frank Zappa**

The End of an Era

Our father died of a heart attack on a Saturday night. It was April 7, 1973. He died at the duplex Frank had purchased for Mom and Dad in North Hollywood on Vantage Avenue.

Frank was doing a show in Arizona and I was at home with our two-year-old son Jason while Marcia was visiting with friends in San Diego.

My sister Candy called and told me that Dad was having a heart attack. I told her to call the paramedics and that I would be there as soon as I could find someone to watch Jason.

While trying to find a sitter my sister called back. "Dad is gone," she said.

His wake was held on Monday April 9. A rosary was said at 7:00 p.m., after which Mom and Frank came to Marcia's and my house for something to eat.

They pulled up in front and I was watching them from the dining room window. When Mom rang the bell I opened the eye-level peephole in the front door.

I had our son's Sesame Street hand puppet, Ernie, on my left hand and held it up to the peephole. Ernie was looking directly at mom. I said, "Who's there?" in my best Ernie voice. Mom and Frank burst out laughing. Humor helped to ease Mom's grief, if only for that brief moment.

The funeral was the following day. Mom was devastated but doing her best to hold it together after Dad's death.

Even though her relationship with Dad was never easy, she loved him. Now she was alone and scared to face the trials of life without him.

Carl and Candy were holding up like troopers. Frank, who had flown in from Arizona, and I were alone with our thoughts about Dad. I tried to think of the good times but it wasn't easy—there were so few to remember.

Only a handful of people attended the graveside gathering. It was sad but a true indication that toward the end of his life, Dad did not have many friends.

Those who did attend had kind things to say about him. Each one said how proud Dad was of Frank and me. That was the first time Frank and I ever heard that. It was a bittersweet revelation, one that would've made our lives better if we had known.

CHAPTER TWENTY-ONE

Final Thoughts...

The relationship that existed between Frank and me during our formative years gradually morphed into a new bond.

The two brothers who had survived so many upheavals by leaning on each other had grown into men who knew they'd always have each other.

It never occurred to me that my brother Frank would leave this earth so soon.

Before he was diagnosed with prostate cancer in 1991, it would've been unimaginable that Frankie and I would be separated so permanently.

No matter how crazy things were around us, we learned to pull together. It was our defense against turmoil and injustices. It was always going to be that way.

Until the day it wasn't.

His death ended a chapter in my life that should have had many more.

Bobby in his coat of many colors in Frankie's studio.

After all that we had been through together—the fights, the friends, the fun, and the stress of the moves—I look back and realize that we made it through all of it because we were brothers and best friends.

With the passing of the years since I left Frank in New York in 1967, I drifted off into my own reality finding a career in the much more sedate business of educational and professional publishing.

Meanwhile, Frank succeeded in reaching the pinnacle in a profession where the odds are about the same as winning the lottery.

I can honestly say that I did not envy his celebrity because he paid dearly for it. The incident in London that nearly cost him his life, the disaster in Montreux, Switzerland; his appearance before the U.S. Senate in defense of the First Amendment; his untimely death from prostate cancer…very few of us who are mere mortals face that much upheaval and certainly not in the public eye.

I knew that my brother was destined to become the Frank Zappa that the world knows. A precious few are born to be great but there was more to his success than just the raw talent he came into the world with.

The events of our early life together played a pivotal role in who he became. Did I contribute to his success?

I can only wish that I did in some small way, but I know for sure that he contributed to mine—and in a big way.

As the eldest son in a Sicilian family with its share of issues, he could've gone in any number of different directions.

I'm so thankful he was able to channel his early life experiences, anger, and stress into the world of art and music. My life is richer for his having been my big brother and I'm still in awe of how much he accomplished.

There was a time when two inseparable brothers knew that the only way they were going to survive the bizarre travails of life was with each other.

Those times made all the difference for both of us and I knew these stories of our youth would die with me unless I found a way to tell them.

I wrote the book so I could share how Frankie and I grew up Zappa and to revisit my question of how two boys from the same family could turn out so differently.

The biggest mystery that remains is how Frank came into the world with either a much higher IQ than others, or an ability to use more of his brain.

No one else in our family seems to have had the intellect that he did. And very few could match his verbal agility and lightning fast assessments.

Aside from our personalities, Frankie and I had distinct roles in our family. As the oldest child, Frank had a completely different experience than I did as the second-to-oldest. That perhaps offers a clue to his strength in leadership abilities.

Our three-year age difference also may explain that our developing minds were at different stages during our frequent moves and how we handled the predicament of never having roots or long-term friendships when we were young.

Another difference between my brother and me was that he had many more health problems than I had. That may help explain how we each perceived the world and how those perceptions determined our reactions.

Frank also had a much higher level of anger than I did and it seems that Frank's anger may have given him the energy to constantly create music and to be able to think faster than most when it came to understanding political and social issues.

When I look back on Frank's relationship with our father, I think there are benchmarks that show how they were alike in so many ways, such as:

- They were both stubborn; neither one gave in without a fight or a test of wills.
- The word "Dictator" comes to mind. Dad demanded obedience at home and Frank demanded obedience in rehearsals, on tour, and on stage.
- They were both willful — they did whatever they wanted to do. I doubt that Frank checked with his wife or kids about going on tour or how much time he spent working on his music
- Frank and Dad constantly came up with new ideas to better themselves; Frank was just much better at it.
- The math and music connection—both activities are obsessive and solitary. Dad's mind was often somewhere else; he was self-absorbed doing math puzzles. Frank was often elsewhere, too, and equally self-

absorbed but with Frank he was creating and solving musical puzzles.

- Dad constantly moved; Frank moved from place to place during all of his music tours

Frank had such a great sense of humor. I bet he'd get a kick out of me comparing him to Dad. Either that or he'd get pissed at me like when I clocked him on the head with the croquet mallet. But he forgave me for that quickly and I think he would for this, too.

Frankie rummaging for food in his Utility Muffin Kitchen.

After writing this memoir, the only thing I know for sure is how much I still miss my brother Frankie. It has been a cathartic experience; it has given me a tremendous sense of relief from the sadness that I have felt on so many occasions over the years since his death by bringing Frank to life again—even if just for this little while.

Writing about him has brought back so many good memories of Frankie and Bobby together again. And, like so many Frank Zappa fans, I'm thankful that Frank lives on through the mountain of music and amazing insights he left behind.

I will always remember Frankie as we were in this picture...

Frankie and Bobby

EPILOGUE

The three friends who went to New York in 1967 to work for Frank Zappa and the Mothers of Invention went their separate ways but have remained the closest of friends for over 50 years. Here's what we've been doing with our lives.

William Henry "Bill" Harris, III

With a style, irreverence, and unmistakable personality all his own, Bill Harris earned his title of "America's #1 Hollywood Reporter" in television, print, and radio, delivering celebrity news and anecdotes, interviews, facts, film reviews, and fun about Hollywood and the stars to an audience of millions, which he's been doing for more than 30 years. As a favorite guest on shows like Oprah, Regis, and Larry King, Bill reached millions more.

Bill's credits range from a remarkable 14 years on-air for "Showtime" to another seven for "E! TV." From years on "Entertainment Tonight" to his daily radio feature on more than 370 radio stations across the United States and over the Armed Forces Radio Network, he's been heard around the world.

For almost 20 years Bill has regularly taken his show biz lectures to sea for cruise lines ranging from Crystal to Holland America. He had his own movie and DVD page in the "National Inquirer" for years. Bill along with Rex Reed spent years hosting the nationally syndicated film review show "At The Movies," which they took over from Siskel and Ebert.

Born in Massachusetts, Bill graduated from Claremont McKenna College and joined a public relations firm, working with stars from Paul Newman to Bob Hope. He wrote the Emmy Award-winning "Ralph Story A.M. Show" for KABC-TV in Los Angeles and then wrote

Rona Barrett's hugely popular daily gossip segments for "Good Morning America" for four years.
They had a most unusual relationship. She fired him three times and he quit twice.

He has written for hosts from Regis Philbin to Florence Henderson and from James Garner to Richard Dawson. There isn't a major screen star he hasn't met and interviewed, and as always shared these interviews with his national television audience.

A resident of the Hollywood Hills, Bill's biggest piece of movie memorabilia is a 95-year old four-level Spanish villa once owned by heartthrob and B-film star Chester Morris, which Bill had restored. Today, his biggest complaint is a lifelong losing battle with striped bass on the island of Nantucket off Cape Cod.

Richard "Dick" Barber

After the most interesting summer of 1967 in New York City with Bobby Zappa and Bill Harris, Richard returned to Southern California to complete his teaching credential and student teaching.

In the spring of 1968, Frank asked if Richard would become his tour manager and oversee his concert tours. Richard happily accepted and began a wild stretch of engrossing—and sometimes catastrophic—years on the road with Frank Zappa and the Mothers of Invention.

One adventure on the road included the raging fire in Montreux, Switzerland set off by a fan's flare during the band's concert, which was memorialized in Deep

Purple's song, "Smoke on the Water." He also made an appearance in the movie "200 Motels" and toured with Linda Ronstadt, The Moody Blues, and Tom Waits.

After eight years of touring with the Mothers, Richard decided to seek a more traditional career path which included selling airplanes and later working as a college administrator. He then focused on the restaurant business.

He established and ran his own restaurant called "Square One" in Claremont, California where he, Bobby, and Bill had grown up.

He also built an airplane, which he has now been flying for the past 24 years. He has flown across the U. S. and throughout the west. After more than a decade in the restaurant business Richard turned to school teaching in Southern California. Then, after a number of years in education, his career focus changed and he took a job driving an 18-wheeler around the country.

Richard then settled in rural Northern Nevada, operating gargantuan earth-moving equipment in Gold and Copper mines. To supplement his income and make use of his formal training as an educator he returned to teaching. In addition to those accomplishments, he built his own house and is now retired. He alternates between spending time in Northern Nevada, Arizona, and Montana.

He also finds time to travel to Europe, Australia, Canada, and the Far East. Friends have encouraged him to write about his diverse career path with emphasis on the numerous adventures "On the road with Frank Zappa and the Mothers." Perhaps one day he will.

Charles Robert "Bobby" Zappa

Photo credit: Journalist Dorri Olds

Frank's brother Bobby graduated from high school in Claremont, California then joined the United States Marine Corps. He served during the Cuban Missile Blockade and in S.E. Asia at the start of the Vietnam War.

After his brief stint working for Frank in the summer of 1967, Bobby earned a bachelor's degree in history from California State Polytechnic University in Pomona, California; a research diploma in social psychology from the University of Stockholm, Sweden; and a master's degree in education from the City University of New York at Lehman College in the Bronx.

In 1975 he moved to New York from Los Angeles to work for publishing giant McGraw-Hill, Inc. He held domestic and international editorial, marketing, and senior management positions in the College Division, the International Division, and a subsidiary company, Datapro Research Corporation with offices in Lausanne, Switzerland.

Later in his career he worked for Prentice-Hall, Maxwell-Macmillan, Simon & Schuster, and Primedia. An avid runner in his early years, Bobby completed the New York City Marathon and the Marine Corps Marathon in Washington, DC. He was formerly Chairman of the College Marketing Committee for the Association of American Publishers and is currently a member of the Waldwick, New Jersey, Police Pistol and Rifle Club.

After leaving publishing in 2002 he joined the New York City Teaching Fellows program to teach at a high school in the South Bronx. He taught U.S. History and economics for 11 years in the New York City public school system at the School for Excellence, one of the five small schools housed in the 110 year-old Morris High School campus building, General Colin Powell's alma mater. In 2011 he was selected to participate in the Congressional Fellow's program for teachers in Washington, DC.

He is now retired and living on the Upper West Side of Manhattan with his wife Diane Papalia.